AFTERMARRIAGE:

The Myth of Divorce

D0981103

AFTERMARRIAGE:

The Myth of Divorce

Unspoken Marriage Agreements and Their Impact on Divorce

Anita Wyzanski Robboy

A Pearson Education Company

This book is dedicated to all my clients, my family, Lucy Cavendish College, Cambridge University, and Professor Jonathan Steinberg.

Copyright © 2002 by Anita Wyzanski Robboy

International Standard Book Number: 0-02-864237-6
Library of Congress Catalog Card Number: 2001094731

04   03   02   8   7   6   5   4   3   2   1

Interpretation of the printing code: The rightmost number of the first series of numbers is the year of the book's printing; the rightmost number of the second series of numbers is the number of the book's printing. For example, a printing code of 02-1 shows that the first printing occurred in 2002.

Printed in the United States of America

Publisher: Marie Butler-Knight
Senior Acquisitions Editor: Renee Wilmeth
Senior Production Editor: Christy Wagner
Product Manager: Phil Kitchel
Managing Editor: Jennifer Chisholm
Copy Editor: Nancy Wagner
Cover Designer: Doug Wilkins
Book Designer: Trina Wurst
Marketing and publicity, contact Dawn Van De Keere, 317-581-3722
International sales and distribution, contact Kit Kemper, 317-581-3665

Contents

Preface

After work, I need to exercise. I know of no better way to cope with the stress, the sadness, and the strangeness of all that I have seen and heard in almost any given day at work.

One day I realized that physical exercise was no longer enough. I could not face all the unhappiness in the ways I previously had. Like a paratrooper who suddenly freezes at the door of the plane and cannot jump, I had seized up. Through a friend, I arranged a sabbatical at Cambridge University, where I intended to write about the legal implications of the new artificial forms of procreation. I took courses, rode my bike, drank tea, and relaxed, but somehow the project never got moving. When people asked about my professional work, I told them stories about the practice of family law and the life of a divorce lawyer. The friend who had arranged the sabbatical suggested that I write about my insights. That casual suggestion changed my life. The result is this book.

Through the words, stories, and thoughts that follow, I hope to convey, at least in small part, what it feels like to engage in the practice of family law. The stories are composites of many clients' stories and do not embody the actual facts of anyone whom I represented. However, the stories are real as measured by the pain, dashed expectations, and problematic situations faced by many who seek the advice of a family lawyer. They show what marriage, divorce, and post-marriage are like for the people involved and the lawyer who is supposed to "fix" everything. The law of divorce can only fix marriage in a very limited and carefully defined manner, circumscribed by the law of marriage.

Acknowledgments

I wish to thank the law firm Casner & Edwards for my sabbatical leave; without time away from the active practice of law, I doubt that I would have had the energy and perspective to create this manuscript. There are many people who inspired, guided, and helped me get to the finish line. I cannot thank them enough or express adequately how grateful I feel for their constant support. The contributions of Professor Jonathan Steinberg, Karen Birdsall, Julie Ingelfinger, Virginia Laplante, and Andrea Maislen were central to the development and shaping of *Aftermarriage*. I am indebted to Phil Kitchel, development editor, for his keen eye and constructive criticism of the draft manuscript, and to Renee Wilmeth, senior acquisitions editor at Alpha Books, who had the courage to select my manuscript for publication. Had Diana Kierein not steered me toward Pearson Technology Group, this book might never have seen the light of day.

I also wish to thank the many friends and family members who faithfully encouraged me and read and reread the drafts I wrote. To name many, and hopefully omit few, I thank my husband, Ed; my daughters, Elizabeth and Caroline; my brother, Charlie; and my relatives, friends, and colleagues: Anita Warburg, Anita and Aleksander Leyfell, Stephanie Warburg, Connie Schnoll and David Rintels, Helen Lee, Lenore Martin, Dhooleka Raj, Ruth Budd, Arlene Bernstein, Julie Ginsburg, Mary Haskell, Marilyn Smith, Gene Dahmen, Jo-Ann Charak Feit, Joel Suttenberg, Karen Tosh, Nancy Lee, Mark Reiff, Ellen Poster, Elizabeth Rogers, Diana Richmond, Shirley Bayle, Greg Englund, and Gerry Ferber. The suggestions of two family court judges, the Honorable Edward M. Ginsburg and the Honorable Herbert H. Hershfang, were invaluable.

CHAPTER 1

Expectations Great and Small

Everyone who contemplates divorce has expectations, great and small, just as they once had expectations for their marriage. Often both sets of expectations come from deeply entrenched but unexamined beliefs. Marital expectations come from a person's culture, religion, law, and, most importantly, from family experiences of the meaning of love, connection, intimacy, marriage, and its endings. From all of these sources comes what I call the *marital construct*. Divorce expectations are inevitably intertwined with a person's individual marital construct. And divorce may occur as the remedy for profound disappointment with unrealistic marital expectations.

The common expectation that spouses will be free of each other after divorce is troublesome and misguided. People expect the divorce process to correct earlier mistakes and to release them from the spouse's infuriating habits, the ill will in the marriage, the lack of trust, and the failure to communicate meaningfully. Persons marrying for the second time are far more sophisticated about marital rights, duties, and obligations, as well as more apprehensive about embarking on the journey again. They also know that divorce does not, in many instances, sever the relationship with a former spouse.

Not only may the divorce not extract a spouse from an unsatisfying relationship, but it also rarely diffuses the intensity of the conflicts between the spouses. Habits and personalities do not change by entering a courthouse. The quality of the relationship between two people does not change as a result of "a day in court," and the judge cannot rebuild trust between the spouses by finding grounds for physical separation. Changing any relationship, particularly where confidence in the other's integrity has been eroded, is enormously difficult. Obtaining a divorce does not build a new or different relationship between the parties; it is merely a symbolic rite of passage, a ceremony without pomp, circumstance, flowers, or food, which will not change people individually or transport them out of the quagmire of their marriage. Building a successful aftermarriage requires diligence and hard work, just as maintaining a successful marriage does—but without the expectations of exclusivity and cohabitation.

As a family lawyer, I meet people who are contemplating marriage, divorce, postdivorce problems, and remarriage. Each couple asks different questions, yet the central themes are similar: "What would change if I were to get married/divorced?" "What can I expect will happen to me financially?" "How can I prepare for the process?" "What do I need to know or be aware of?" Even as I hear these questions, I know that the person asking them has some ideas of his or her own as to what will, should, or might happen.

Most people planning to marry for the first time do not comprehend the meaning of marriage within the law. They have some familiarity with its cultural significance and its religious meanings, but not the legal implications. Prospective divorce clients are no better informed. They ask: "How can I end my marriage?" "How can I have nothing to do with my spouse?"

"How long will the process take?" "When can I start to date?" or "Can I move out of state?"

During the initial consultation, I ask, "What is your best fantasy as to what will happen? How do you want things to be in the future?"—questions designed to gauge whether the person has realistic expectations of what the law can and cannot do for him or her. I hear all kinds of answers, such as: "If my spouse would change, I would not want a divorce ... I cannot stand the abusive way he treats me ... I want to be with someone I can love and trust ... I want never to see or hear from him (or her) ... I want the person out of my life and out of my children's lives."

Unfortunately, the piece of paper titled "Decree of Divorce Nisi" is not a ticket out of the obligations and duties of marriage. Little will really change as a result of the divorce, and certainly far less than many had hoped. As one family court judge always tells parties at the close of their hearing, "You are no longer husband and wife, but you are parents forever."

Nearly every divorcing person has the fantasy that his or her partner will be shed. Persons who have had long marriages or marriages with children will never be able to shed their partners like a chrysalis. They will have a thousand points of connection in the future because of their children, their financial obligations to each other, and their history.

In effect, all that the divorce process really can do is rearrange the place of the "other" in their lives; it will not eradicate the connection or the experience. Only in childless, short marriages can there be a complete disengagement. Such marriages are more truly affairs, which leave the parties without everlasting connections. In almost all other marriages, such termination is illusory. Marriages never really end. The partners simply rearrange themselves; they become two people who live at different addresses, with possibly, but not necessarily, a more attenuated attachment. Some link remains, whether negative, positive, ambivalent, or a combination of all, varying over time and even at any particular time. Decades after the children are grown and decades after the parties divorce, issues such as the right to retire, the appropriateness of continued support, and division of retirement benefits and/or pension may arise, as well as concerns about illness and life insurance benefits.

What follows divorce, then, is the period I call *after-marriage*. Where couples have had children together, they will have a lifetime of caring about each other's existence, perhaps not directly or consciously for their own sakes, but for their children's. After long marriages, the habits of thinking as part of a couple dissolve only over time. Anger may expedite the process of dissolution, but it will not obliterate the power of a lengthy history together. No divorce can rewrite history.

The myths of divorce raise unrealistic expectations for divorcing couples. The legal documents may declare that the couple is living apart for justifiable cause or, alternatively, that there are "grounds" for the parties to have separated, perhaps that "the marriage is irretrievably broken down." The latter is also a legal fiction, as a physicist client of mine pointed out when he refused to proceed with a divorce on the ground of irretrievable breakdown, arguing rightfully that he did not know whether the marriage had broken down "irretrievably" and for all time or only temporarily. He believed his wife still loved him, as he so clearly loved her, and that in the ripeness of time she would come to appreciate and reexperience her affection for him.

The purpose of this book is to introduce a new under-standing of the meaning of marriage and divorce. I have found that the bonds of matrimony in many types of marriages endure until death. Seeing divorce as a part of marriage is more legally accurate than seeing divorce as a final curtain call to the marriage performance. After cohabiting marriage has ended, husband and wife enter the state of aftermarriage.

Redefining the expectations of divorce to include the state of aftermarriage creates a climate in which parties can make the transition more smoothly from an intact marriage to a situation of continued marital obligations and duties, coupled with an ongoing relationship but without the right to physical proximity. It also highlights the long shadow cast by the original marriage contract which, while amended, cannot be expunged in its entirety. What follows are the stories of people who chose wisely, or unwisely, in light of aftermarriage. They cover the marital experience from people's first prenuptial introduction to the possibility of divorce, through the divorce process itself, to the condition of aftermarriage and including even remarriage.

This book will assist people in traveling from the land of marriage to the land of aftermarriage in the least harmful way possible. There are no road maps as such, but there are pathways to avoid. Some of the traps awaiting divorcing couples can be predicted from the type of marriage that they have had. I believe that marriages can be loosely categorized, providing signposts along the journey from marriage to aftermarriage. What distinguishes one category from another are the unspoken agreements that exist in all marriages.

The Unspoken Agreements of Marriage

Until people are dealing with divorce, they think they understand the meaning of marriage. The concept of marriage sounds straightforward and simple as written in the statute. However, the unraveling of a marriage causes bizarre and unanticipated consequences, one being the redefinition of the real meaning of the marriage bargain.

People are unprepared for the long reach of the institution of marriage. When parties marry, the state has, in effect, joined in their union, and the concerns of the state and society at large cannot be dismissed lightly. The "protections of marriage," the duties and obligations of the spouses, have institutional backing, irrespective of desire to sever the relationship. Although married people gain many benefits by marriage, such as preferential health insurance, life insurance, pension and retirement benefits, Social Security, and possible tax benefits, to name but a few, they have lost the right to self-determination and privacy.

People also do not expect that marriage has categories or types. Those expectations from our culture, our family, and our understanding of love and marriage, as well as our individual circumstances of finances, careers, and children, are all the terms of what I call the *marriage bargain*. People do not think much about the nature of their marriage or the terms of their marital bargain when they are happily married; it only comes up when, if, and as unhappiness grows. As Tolstoy wrote so aptly as the first sentence of his famous book, *Anna Karenina,* "ALL happy families are like one another; each unhappy family is unhappy in its own way."

When divorcing, people expect the outcome of divorce to reflect how the partners behaved during the marriage and what each one contributed, or failed to contribute, to the marriage. How should unhappiness be measured? How can one measure the damages of a failed marriage? The dissolution of a marriage makes it the court's job to identify and place value on the terms of the marriage bargain—a bargain that in many cases the parties did not consciously strike! Trying to do so is the source of enormous pain, litigation, and legal fees, as lawyers and the court inquire into the circumstances of the marriage. What was the "deal" of the marriage? Were the people really partners? Were they *equal* partners? What did they promise to do for each other and the family? What *did* they do for each other? Who was the homemaker and raised the children?

In determining what is fair, the court considers a host of factors in the couple's marital history, encompassing their present and past situation, as well as their anticipated future lifestyle had they stayed together. The factors enumerated in most divorce statutes include some, if not all, of the following factors about the divorcing couple: length of the marriage, age, health, lifestyle, financial incomes of the parties (past, present, and future), employability, opportunity to acquire future assets and income, past contributions (financial and nonfinancial), needs of the parties, needs of the children (financial, educational, medical, and special), and homemaking.

These fine distinctions become important when a marriage is in the process of dissolution because any judgment or decision is based on the facts presented at trial, which give human form and individual character to the statutory factors that the judge must consider. The facts presented to a judge derive from the story of the marriage as told by each of the spouses, the expert witnesses, and other witnesses called by each party's lawyers. A lawyer also collects the story of the children, the financial story, and the stories not told—the "secret" stories of the family, the partners, or an individual family member.

The spouses' stories are never the same, although there may be events to which they both refer and allusions to the same difficulties. There are no true "facts," only experiences, which, like dreams, have reference points, common elements characterizing the marital history, and the parties' marital bargain.

The Types of Marital Bargains

Although each marital bargain is unique, in my experience, certain stories come up again and again, allowing us to form categories of marriage.

Let me emphasize that the categories I outline in this chapter, and illustrate in the chapters that follow, are my own very personal way of analyzing the many types of marriages that I have watched unravel. They do not mirror the language used in court decisions or legal textbooks. They are intended as useful *handles* for people to think differently about marriage, marital partnerships, the marriage contract, their own personal marital construct, and aftermarriage. Understanding the original (and actually lived) marital bargain offers a basis for predicting what may happen in aftermarriage.

There tend to be five types of marriages or marriage bargains that become evident upon divorce. Each category of marriage has a distinct marital bargain as its hallmark. The five types of marital bargains are as follows: the *classic marriage bargain,* the *companion marriage bargain,* the *protectorate marriage bargain,* the *complex marriage bargain,* and the *failed affair/childless, short marriage.*

In the classic marriage bargain, the husband is the primary wage earner and provider, and the wife is the primary homemaker and parent responsible for raising the children. In the companion marriage bargain, the spouses are equal partners (and parents) and expect to be each other's best friend. Protectorate marriage bargains are between unequal spouses: one spouse assumes the responsibility of protecting the other in return for the adoration of the protected party. In the extramarital or complex marital bargain, an extra entity, person, or constellation of persons are vital to sustaining the marriage.

Only in the fifth type of marriage, failed affair/childless, short marriage, is there no need for realignment in aftermarriage. In this type of marriage, divorce is, in fact, the end of all marital business. Upon divorce, there is hardly any disengagement to engineer. The couple's relationship is like two ships that sailed together for a while and then, during the night, took separate courses. There is no residual baggage or legally enforceable marital duty that requires the couple to have continuing contact. A childless, short marriage is often a first marriage between people in their twenties or thirties. The couple, intentionally or unintentionally, maintain separate assets and liabilities. No property is acquired jointly, except perhaps a house and some furniture or perhaps only a pet. Each is employed, and neither one is looking to the other for support.

In contract language, one would say that there had been no consideration for the marriage because neither gave up something, nor refrained from doing something, for the other. In partnership language, one might say they lacked or did not reach a partnership goal (such as children) and simply carried on with their lives as before, but under a common roof.

If one spouse gave up his or her job and relocated and then was unable to find comparable employment, a judge might consider the situation more sympathetically, especially if the employed spouse had sufficient means to compensate the unemployed spouse. However, the most common outcome of divorce after this type of marriage is that the jointly held assets are divided equally, and the remaining assets and liabilities are left with whoever owns them.

Our Cast of Characters

In Chapter 2, "Understanding the Marital Construct," you will meet three individuals who are facing situations that require them to think about their own individual marital constructs. Suzanne is planning to marry for the first time. Charlie is planning to remarry. Helen is considering leaving her marriage.

Beginning with Chapter 3, "The Classic Marriage Bargain," and continuing throughout the book, you will be introduced to five divorcing couples. Their stories illustrate the marital bargain types that *will,* for various reasons, entail an aftermarriage. You will see how the couples chose, wisely or unwisely, their paths through the marital experience, from first introduction, to the possibility of divorce, through the divorce process, to the aftermarriage, and even on to subsequent marriages.

In Chapter 3, you will come to know two couples who have classic marriage bargains: Mary Ann and Vin and Henry and Eleanor. Mary Ann and Vin will illustrate how, at every crossroad, they chose paths that maximized their pain and conflict. In contrast, Henry and Eleanor will exemplify a couple who came to the divorce process with more realistic expectations and managed to remain constructively focused. Natalie and Martin, introduced in Chapter 4, are involved in a companion marriage, where the major issue is how they share their children. The fourth couple, Bettina and Mark, first appear in Chapter 5. They are involved in a protectorate marriage bargain. The fifth and last couple are Ginny and Zack, introduced in Chapter 6. They are involved in a complex marriage bargain.

The five couples' stories will illustrate not only different marriage bargains but the terrain people cross from marriage to aftermarriage. The paths of mediation, negotiation, and litigation will be discussed, all in the context of this cast of five couples. You will read scenes that describe how these couples negotiate their divorces and what going to court was like for Mary Ann and Vin. The couples' lives will not stop with the day of their divorce hearing because that day did not mark the end of their relationship. The last chapter of this book will describe their lives in aftermarriage, a time span far longer than any couple's divorce process.

CHAPTER 2

Understanding the Marital Construct

Understanding that divorce is a phase of marriage reframes expectations of what will happen after spouses physically separate. The expectations of divorce, and hence of aftermarriage, derive from the expectations and assumptions about marriage that I have called the *marital construct*.

My window into a person's understanding of marriage opens whenever I help a couple craft a prenuptial agreement, a contract between a man and woman who intend to be married. Its purpose is to alter the marital relationship created by the laws of marriage. For many people, the process is a startling learning experience. Clients tell me they had not realized what marriage laws say about marriage and the marital relationship upon divorce. Suzanne and Paul's story illustrates some common assumptions and misconceptions of young people marrying for the first time.

First Marriage: Suzanne and Paul

Suzanne and Paul were to be married in July in an elaborate wedding at a grand hotel in a major city with over 400 guests. Suzanne, 24, had recently finished a master's degree in art history and was looking for a job, hard to find in her field of study given the market. Paul, 25, was hoping for a job on Wall Street when he finished his MBA in the spring. Suzanne was thrilled to be engaged to Paul and had never been happier in her life. Suzanne's parents liked Paul well enough, though he was not exceptionally bright or handsome, not as "special" as they had wanted for their daughter. Paul was personable, but it was true that he did not seem marked for outstanding success and, perhaps, was a "catch" only in Suzanne's eyes. However, he was enormously kind and even-tempered, not overly greedy or ambitious. Suzanne's parents knew that they could only celebrate their daughter's happiness.

However, Suzanne's parents did insist that she and Paul needed a prenuptial agreement, given the enormous disparity in their financial circumstances. Suzanne was already worth nearly two million dollars, and, when she reached her thirtieth birthday, she was destined to receive another portion of her great-grandmother's trust. Suzanne had an inkling of this, but no detailed knowledge and even less curiosity. She preferred not to know, as she already felt guilty about having so much more money than nearly all her friends and her beloved Paul. She never asked her parents about their wealth, and the entire family preferred not to discuss the subject.

Suzanne's parents wanted their daughter to have a prenuptial agreement to prevent the predictable operation of the laws of marriage and divorce. They wanted Paul fenced off from claiming any property that Suzanne had, or would receive, from her family in the event of divorce.

Paul and Suzanne had talked about where they hoped to live after Paul graduated and how they wanted to get a dog. However, they had not discussed how they would handle money matters in their marriage. That topic only arose sporadically over restaurant bills, expensive theatre tickets, or hotel accommodations on weekend vacations. They had been comfortable sharing big-ticket expenses and alternating smaller ones, and they never talked about whether they would have a joint checking account when they married. Suzanne and Paul had expectations as to how money in marriage should be handled but had never discussed them. They hoped to have a family in a few years, after Paul was established on Wall Street. Suzanne was glad to have time to travel with Paul and work for a few years before having children.

They were excited to be looking at apartments together and planning their honeymoon. Suzanne's parents' request was "so inconvenient," and Suzanne hated having to ask Paul to "do this anti-romantic legal thing." She was mortified and wished her parents were not so insistent, but that was how they were, and they were paying for the wedding.

Suzanne and Paul were like many young couples in the way they each romanticized marriage. Neither one considered their pending nuptials as a contract and a partnership. They were only aware that a minister would officiate at the ceremony in his religious capacity. Suzanne and Paul did not truly understand the significance of obtaining a license to marry, although they did realize that marriage laws impacted their relationship with regard to money matters, individual and joint assets, and debts. A government or city's sanctioning their marriage meant that they had agreed to the State becoming a silent partner in their relationship. The terms and conditions of marriage were a matter of applicable state laws. Knowledge and consent are not a precondition to their applicability.

Married people are considered equal partners who have entered into a marital contract. That contract provides that the partners will support and maintain each other in life and provide for the surviving spouse's support and maintenance after death. Married people owe each other the implied duty of good faith and fair dealing.

My first meeting with Suzanne occurred in late May. She informed me of her wedding plans, the difficulty of getting a large hotel, and her parents' request that she enter into a prenuptial agreement. Thus began the task of negotiating between "Cupid and the Devil," the essence of what lawyers face when asked to represent a party seeking a premarital contract with his, or her, beloved. I began by explaining that prenuptial agreements are designed to address two circumstances in particular: what happens if the couple divorces and what happens when one of them dies.

The prenuptial agreement is a legal document that eliminates or foreshortens a spouse's obligation of support and/or eliminates or reduces any obligation to share present or future property interests. The usual types of property that people try to protect are inheritances, expectancies, or property that a person owns prior to marriage. An interest in a family business is a common subject of protection. To be valid and enforceable, the premarital agreement must be entered into freely and voluntarily, without fraud or duress. As the premarital contract is by definition a document that devilishly limits the protective effects of the marriage laws, a person should sign one only after receiving legal advice. The draconian consequences of the premarital contract may not be legally enforceable if a spouse has not had the benefit of counsel before waiving those marital rights. Furthermore, and most importantly, a prenuptial agreement is only enforceable later if full and complete financial disclosure preceded the waiving of rights. Suzanne's present and future expectations of wealth must be accurately conveyed to Paul and his counsel. The lack of duress at the time of signing the prenuptial agreement can be documented at a later time by reference to a protracted history of negotiations prior to the wedding.

Suzanne looked aghast. She coughed, paused, then smiled and said, "I have absolute trust in Paul. He loves me and does not want my parents' money. My parents even like him, or at least they act as if they do. What would happen if we didn't do this?"

I answered, "If you don't have a premarital agreement, Paul, as your husband, will have the automatic right in this state—and many, but not all, other states—to claim an interest in your inherited and family property. A spouse upon marriage and divorce has a legal right to claim an interest in all marital property whenever, however, and wherever acquired. The trust property created for you by your grandparents is an asset that your husband could seek a share of under the laws of marriage and divorce. While you know that he has no desire or wish to do so, your parents want to make sure that he will never be able to ask for any part of your family's wealth."

Suzanne's legal education was about to begin. The romance of lovers would now be transmuted into an understanding that the law considers marriage to be a business arrangement, a partnership, governed by a contract that states the rights, duties, and obligations of the partners. The lessons of the law would splash cold water on Suzanne's warm, fuzzy, trusting feelings toward Paul.

I eased into my tutorial. The Common Law, which originated in England and was the foundation of American law, granted married women no separate legal rights. A married woman had no right to own land apart from her husband, and all profit from her land and other goods belonged exclusively to her husband. Children were considered chattel, a form of property. This early formulation of the legal relationship of married men and women has been substantially modified and corrected in the twentieth century. Married men and women have equal rights in parenthood, in real and personal property ownership, and in inheritance laws.

However, the vestiges of the myth of two becoming one by marriage has persisted in crevices of the law. The current vestige can be found in the legal fiction of marriage as a partnership of two equal partners. A partnership is a unique, well-defined, discreet legal entity. It is different from any other legal entity such as an individual, a corporation, or a trust. Marital partners are presumed to be equal partners who owe a fiduciary duty toward the other. There are express (clearly stated) laws governing behavior, such as the duty of support. And there are implied duties (not stated, but inferred), such as the duty of good faith, fair dealing, and sexual fidelity. The laws of marriage and inheritance create a partnership that endures throughout life and even after death. The law presumes that married people want their surviving spouse and children, if any, to receive their estate if no will exists. Even a disinherited spouse has the right as a surviving partner to demand her share of the partnership by asserting her "forced share."

A couple who want to alter the arrangements presumed by the law must do so proactively. A will is such an instrument in the context of death. A prenuptial agreement is the legal instrument used to alter legally enforceable marriage expectations.

I noticed with relief that Suzanne was attentive and seemed to understand she needed to know what I was telling her. She said, "I had no idea that women used to have no rights to property upon marriage or that marriage is now considered an equal partnership. Did that happen as a result of the women's movement?"

I responded, "Yes, and the amazing fact is how little the law relating to women's rights had changed before the second half of the twentieth century. When I began practicing law, alimony was only for women, and men were not entitled to support under any circumstances. Today, and for the past several decades, all alimony statutes are gender neutral."

When Suzanne said, "I thought alimony was always for whoever needed support," it was time to move on to the next lesson, which was to explain to her some further terms of partnership and contract law.

Historically, the purpose of the marital partnership and contract of marriage was the procreation and protection of children. This remains unchanged, even though some people prefer to think of marriage merely as a statement of love. Partnership law provides that partners have an undivided interest in the whole partnership property and are jointly and separately liable for partnership debt. There are no assigned boundaries within the whole, or to say it another way, nothing belongs exclusively to one partner. Marriage merges all property, regardless of whether the partners intend it. Regardless of who holds title to a specific piece of property, all property acquired during marriage is considered marital property, except in community property states where inherited property is excluded. Property owned prior to marriage is considered marital property, except in community property states where premarital property is distinguished from post-marital property.

Our state statute provides that all property, wherever, however, and whenever obtained, is marital property, meaning everything owned by a married person is subject to division upon divorce or death. Upon marriage, Paul would have the right to make a claim to all monies presently held in Suzanne's name by virtue of the union they were about to legally forge. Were they to separate and divorce, he would have the right to claim an interest in monies Suzanne had received from her family. After a short marriage, Paul's claim would be far weaker than if they were to divorce after 30 years. The longer the partnership lasts, the more likely that some of the inherited or once-separate monies will be shared. How Suzanne and Paul used her trust income and principal may also become very important in a later division. Were they to buy a house with money that was originally in a trust fund for Suzanne's benefit only and place her name and Paul's on the deed to the house, Paul might well later say that she had made a gift to him of half of its value. Where trust monies have been woven into the fabric of a family's lifestyle, a person may be later prevented from claiming that it is not a family resource. This can be seen, for example, when a judge finds that rearrangement of the family is not a basis for disrupting a child who receives private schooling paid by a parent's trust fund.

The second concept central to understanding the laws of marriage is that the act of marriage creates not only a partnership but also a contract between husband and wife. I asked Suzanne if she knew that she and Paul needed a marriage license, the legal proof of a valid marriage. She said they were in the process of getting one—they had already inquired about blood tests, a prerequisite for a marriage license.

I said, "The marriage license is the legal document that provides written proof that you are, in fact, married. There's no fine print on it that spells out the terms and conditions, but it is the marital contract!"

Suzanne looked perplexed and then said, "Paul and I met last week with the minister. He said that he would be preparing a form for us, with our names and the place we will be married. Is that what you mean?"

I explained that the minister has the authority to grant a religious marriage but not necessarily a civil one, although nearly every minister, priest, and rabbi who applies for civil authority is granted it. The document the minister would prepare proved only that a religious ceremony had taken place; the city or town where the newlyweds would marry must provide the civil documentation of legitimacy. A marriage license is a civil, not religious, document.

Suzanne said that even though the minister had not told them about the difference between a religious and a civil marriage, he had given them a religious perspective on marriage. I asked her what she had learned. She withdrew a small scrap of paper from her purse and said, "The first mention of marriage is in the Bible, Genesis, Chapter 2, Verse 23, 'And Adam said, this is now bone of my bones and flesh of my flesh; she shall be called Woman because she was taken of Man.' And the second mention is in the next paragraph, 'Therefore shall a man leave his father and mother and cleave unto his wife: and they shall be one flesh.'"

Impressed with Suzanne's knowledge and memory, I explained that the legal concept of marriage is derived from the religious one. The Common Law adopted the concept of the unity and oneness of the couple in marriage from the religious one. In early England, the Crown, in an effort to gain power, made marriage a civil ceremony. Only in the twentieth century has the law of marriage been transmuted yet again by grafting principles of partnership law onto the relationship of husband and wife. The earlier religious belief that a married couple was "one flesh" has persisted in romantic beliefs surrounding marriage and in recast marriage expectations.

The marriage license is a contract. The legally enforceable marriage contract creates explicit obligations of support and maintenance, regardless of the location of the spouses. The duty to support a spouse endures throughout life and in death; it is only partially terminated by the divorce process. Failure to support a spouse and/or children subjects the payer-spouse to civil and/or criminal penalties. The right of sexual intimacy between a husband and a wife is eliminated only when a court has determined that a couple is living apart for "justifiable cause." Until then, the crime of adultery may be charged. The failure to consummate a marriage is a grounds for divorce in every civil statute and even in religious law. The Catholic Church, while not recognizing the legitimacy of divorce, does grant an annulment on the grounds of failure to consummate a marriage.

I was delighted with Suzanne's keen intelligence and poise as she said, "How can I promise to take care of Paul but still honor my parents' request that I protect the money they gave me? You know, I really don't think of it as my money. I hold it in trust for my parents, or perhaps my children, if Paul and I have children. What do you suggest the contract should say? I just want to do whatever will please my parents and not offend Paul."

Before we talked about the terms of her initial offer, I cautioned Suzanne that a prenuptial agreement can always be challenged on the basis of a judicial finding of duress, fraud, or a finding that the premarital agreement was unconscionable. A prenuptial agreement is evaluated by a judicial process only when one party seeks to enforce its terms. At that point—years after it was signed—a court must determine that it was not unconscionable when entered into or in the spouses' current financial circumstances. Every premarital contract carries the risk of later unenforceability and, of course, the risk of inaccurately predicting the financial future. I suggested that Suzanne and Paul talk about her parents' difficult request after he had met with his lawyer.

As a general guideline, I suggested that Suzanne pay Paul an amount that increases with each year of marriage. That sum could be reasonably generous considering her feelings and attitude. A possible sum to start with might be around $50,000 in year one, $100,000 in year two, and so on, climbing by $50,000 per year up to a maximum of $500,000 dollars after 10 years of marriage. A similar approach could be reasonable with respect to what amount he should receive were she to die first. Also, Suzanne could always make a will that would override the provisions of the prenuptial agreement, and they could always by agreement declare the prenuptial agreement null and void.

I admitted to Suzanne that I find premarital agreements very troublesome. In my experience, they are no guarantee of the avoidance of future litigation. In fact, they often provoke litigation. However, in Suzanne's circumstances, I was sympathetic with her parents' concern and her desire to please them despite being in a position she personally found compromising.

Suzanne's situation was not that unusual, although it was peculiar for her. Her parents were actually the people invested in this endeavor, not the young woman in my office. Nevertheless, after a normal amount of pushing and pulling between the lawyers, all while Suzanne's parents watched like hawks perched on twin tree-tops, a prenuptial agreement was signed and well in advance of the wedding date. The agreement was never challenged; the couple's marriage flourished, and each found great joy and solace in the marital relationship.

Remarriage: Charlie

Previously married people who plan to remarry often seek advice about whether they ought to consider a prenuptial agreement. These requests usually come in a very different context from younger people marrying for the first time. Previously widowed or divorced people often have children to protect in life and after death. They may have a former spouse to whom they pay alimony or for whom they maintain health and life insurance. Charlie's remarriage presents another perspective on prenuptial agreements and on marriage expectations.

Charlie insisted on a prenuptial agreement with his second wife. He had not had one with his first wife, and less than two years ago I had represented him in his divorce. He was much older and wiser now about the import of marriage. He knew that he wanted the protection of a prenuptial agreement, and he knew the process of preparing and negotiating it would force his new fiancée and him to have a full discussion of marriage expectations, especially financial questions. He thought, admittedly cynically, that it might serve as a preview of how they would behave should they ever negotiate *their* divorce settlement. He and his intended had never fully explored how they would handle the obligation of support if either one were seriously incapacitated, only how they would manage anticipated lifecycle changes such as child rearing.

Charlie's expectations of marriage had changed radically. He now understood the contractual nature of the commitment, the meaning of the law of marriage, and the horror of divorce. He was determined to make his second marriage work, and he wanted to lay a solid foundation for its success. He wanted to be careful to ensure a fit of internal landscapes, focusing on how they handled their disagreements. He was far less concerned with his partner's appearance and charm than when he had been younger. He wanted to spell out, in advance, the purposes for proceeding toward a committed relationship in which the State had an interest. He wanted to curtail the marital obligation of spousal support and ensure that all his premarital property remained exclusively his if there were an aftermarriage.

In short, he was far more cautious, calculating, and introspective in approaching his second marriage. He knew that he was choosing "coupling" with its intrinsic restrictions, benefits, and joys. He also was choosing parenthood, and that was the prime motivating force for him. He wanted his wife to be a mother first and foremost; having a companion was secondary to him.

Charlie knew the marriage-failure rate of 40 to 50 percent. He knew that the chances of success were even lower the second time, reflecting the complexity of arriving at remarriage with internal *and* external baggage. Remarriage is *always* a "complex" bargain, as the former spouse is the third leg of the stool, especially when there are children. While the formerly married group may have superior knowledge of the legal ramifications of marriage, they also have a richer, more textured past than previously, and the challenge of the situation is far greater. Even if Charlie's choice the second time is a wiser one, any second marriage is fraught with internal and external complexity.

Realistic expectations of the difficulties of a complex remarriage can fortify an individual. Whenever I represent someone who is planning to marry someone who was previously married, I caution them about the inevitable scars of the first marriage, so evident in the process of preparing a prenuptial agreement. I counsel my novice client that knowledge of the underbelly of marriage can cause fears that need to be handled gently and carefully. Couples who are forewarned may be able to take the rejection or withdrawal caused by those fears less personally and, more importantly, not respond by trying to fix the partner.

Consultation with Helen

Another window into people's marital construct happens when I meet with a husband or wife who wants a consultation about divorce. While expressing dissatisfaction with the marriage, the unhappy spouse also states that he or she is not ready for physical separation and certainly not divorce. I often speculate to myself what might differentiate these people from those who segue from marriage to aftermarriage.

Helen came to my office late in the afternoon, having left early from the hospital where she is an attending physician in dermatology. Her long days are followed by short evenings with her husband and three children. She was tortured with worry and fear that her husband, also a physician, would leave her for a nurse with whom he worked and with whom he had had an intermittent affair. On several occasions, Helen and her husband had talked about this. It had troubled her before, and it was gnawing at her again, even though her husband had assured her that he very much loved her and would not leave the marriage. Helen was uncertain of her husband's credibility, no matter what he said. But what most deeply anguished Helen was her own confusion about how to respond, what action to take, if any. Her consultation was her effort to become informed about what her life might look like if she obtained a divorce.

"Am I just waiting for the other shoe to drop?" Helen wondered in our conference. I could sense that she still deeply loved her husband, but she could not square her attachment with her outrage at his shallow marital commitment. How could she allow herself to be with a man who would behave as he had? What had happened to her values and sense of self-worth? Or was she asking a question that did not matter?

Helen's dilemma was causing her to weigh and measure her marital construct and her aftermarriage marital construct. I listen as she tells me of her painful situation and confusion. I can, and do, answer the objective, legal parts of her questions. I describe for her the box of reasonable settlement, the statistics of peaceful settlement, the ways people share children, and the like. The two horns of her dilemma call for a subjective judgment, and I am powerless to give her truly comforting answers. They will have to come from inside her.

Origin of Marital Expectations

Where do ideas about marriage begin, and how are they formed? I believe individuals derive their concept of marriage from religious beliefs, cultural beliefs, and definitions provided by the law. Finally, and most importantly, their ideas of marriage come from their experience of their family understanding of what marriage means, as perceived by their own personality and character. Helen is unlikely to find her dilemma lightened by my chatter about marriage as a partnership of equals who have entered, wittingly or unwittingly, into a contract. Her religious beliefs may guide her toward one path or another, but not allay her self-doubt, I suspect. A social anthropological perspective may help her remember that marriages were not always the basic unit for raising children. Definitions of what constitutes family, household, and marriage are products of local culture. Yet this type of academic knowledge is unlikely to be central to her decision.

People who stay married do so because their marital construct is flexible. If Helen stays in her marriage, it will be because she has redefined her marital construct and worked out with her husband a means of aligning their concepts of an acceptable marriage. Had they had wholly compatible definitions, her marriage experience might have been less jagged. The expectation that marriages have ages and stages is important. Marriages move from health to "illness" and then forward through recovery to a state of renewed health, with some residual complications.

Helen may choose to accept less alignment and stability than she had bargained for. More sadly and unexpectedly, Helen may have to accept less than she would have wished for and more disappointment than she would have earlier thought acceptable.

Couples who remain married have had to design and redesign their marital constructs many times. In effect, they marry and remarry and remarry. Very few marriage arrangements remain constant over time. A flexible marital construct anticipates that over time the partners may need to perform unanticipated roles in the relationship. Even when there are disappointments, there is still satisfaction in knowing that with this mate, no other arrangement would have been possible.

Family of Origin Understanding of Marriage

Every individual comes to marriage with an understanding of what marriage means based on his or her family's interpretation of the marriage relationship. The first and most intimate encounters of what love and partnership mean are derived from watching our parents interact. We have absorbed the joy and perhaps cost of interdependency. We have learned that equal may mean "equal," or it may mean "voiceless" if not attached to any source of earned income. Or perhaps we have learned that what women want is important in some circumstances and what men want is important in others. In some parental models, the female partner is the dominant force and the male is subservient, regardless of monetary contribution. In others, the couple negotiates all areas of their lives as equals and no power struggles exist.

Our understanding of intimacy and closeness has its origin in how love was expressed, if at all, in our families. In some families, caring is expressed by criticism, closeness by verbal attention. Silence is used as a weapon. The patterns of emotional connection among families vary enormously, and whatever was practiced in the family of origin is incorporated into a person's marital construct. This is often unconscious and extremely difficult to access, much less verbalize to a fiancé or marriage partner. Yet the baggage of the past has branded an individual's expectations and formed a set of responses, even if they are disguised with practice and over time. The often inaccessible and buried assumptions and presumptions of the family of origin's method of relating influence an individual's marital style and marital construct.

The particular and peculiar personal aspect of the marital construct is also, and most importantly, a product of personality and character through which all information and experience are filtered. The definition and importance of loyalty in a person's value scheme is an example. The definition and importance of relating or coupling is another example. Personality and character may determine whether we have an internal need to couple or not. Some of us will couple regardless of the circumstance because of a compulsive need to experience ourselves in the context of, or in relation to, another. Others may not have such a need, but may choose a partner because of external circumstances or pressures, such as the desire to have children, or because of a chance encounter with someone who simply changes their life.

Mixed Marriages

I believe that all marriages are mixed marriages. No two people hold the identical expectation of marriage or concept of marriage, regardless of their background or their familiarity with the institution. Even when there are no apparent religious, cultural, or social differences, there is no single marital construct. Every person carries a marital construct that is peculiar, personal, and variable depending upon one's particular stage of life.

Spouses are hardly ever in the same stage or phase of the marriage experience, even if they may appear to be so for a brief period.

What I do know is that couples need to speak to each other, make explicit their peculiar and personal marital construct with each other, and share their understanding of marriage. After having done so, they may then be able to merge their distinct models into a single workable version. This process must be repeated throughout a marriage if it is to endure. If merging becomes an impossibility, the couple needs to respect and honor their irreconcilable differences. Doing so requires realignment of their marital constructs, because the expectation of a shared marital construct can no longer be met.

Couples who have been married many years know that their marriage has actually been many marriages. They realign their marital constructs time and again to forge a new alliance with new contours. A change in employment may cause the other spouse to become the major or minor breadwinner. Such a shift requires flexibility and adaptability, since with "the purse" may go the power and control in the relationship. Who is the more available parent to the children can be a result of economic circumstance rather than active planning.

Marriage as an Ideal

Redefining or realigning the marital construct may not always be appropriate. The circumstances may be beyond or outside even the most flexible and forgiving marital construct. I would remind someone like Helen, who is struggling with disappointment and sadness, that the idea of monogamous marriage until death is a combination of that which a person idealizes and that which a person can actualize. The law embodies a Platonic view of marriage. The construct of marriage seeks to memorialize this duality: the reality of life as lived and the ideals to which humanity aspires. A committed, totally satisfactory, monogamous, lifelong marriage is a Platonic ideal. The marriage design inspires human beings to reach beyond any realistic grasp because in doing so the spirit of mankind is ennobled. Religious traditions, where the sanctity of marriage originated as a concept and ceremony, have also combined the reality with a compelling fantasy of the holiness of the union of man and woman in marriage.

Why Do Some Marriages Unravel?

One's understanding of the experiences of marriage, divorce, and aftermarriage is an organic, evolving phenomenon; it is a work in progress, even when that "progress" feels more like regression. Just as a successful marriage is said to require hard work, so, too, do a successful divorce and aftermarriage. Examination and re-examination of one's perceptions are crucial. With time and experience apart, those perceptions will change and bring new understanding. The benefits and burdens of associating with a former spouse may be calibrated differently at different times, especially when viewed after intervening experiences, less intimacy, and greater reflection.

Why do people divorce, given the grim realities? Is it that they do not know what their lives will be like after divorce, or is it that they expect too much from marriage? Why do people march headlong toward divorce irrespective of the emotional, psychological, and financial costs? Why do some people in equally grim circumstances never consider divorce? What makes one person shy away from the process but not another in similar circumstances of loneliness, betrayal, distrust, or disappointment?

I have often wondered about the answers to these questions. The story the client tells me, the story I tell the court, the story I hear from the other spouse, the secret stories, and the financial tales are not sufficient to answer why one of the parties elects divorce as the solution to "the problem" (and only one need do so). I have developed some theories about the critical differences between those who choose to proceed to divorce and those who recommit to their marriage after a crisis or, at the very least, accept the *status quo*.

Couples who stay together after disappointment and/or betrayal individually determine to recommit themselves to the marriage. In effect, couples who stay together marry and remarry many times over in the course of their years together. There are very few couples in which one or both partners have not experienced disappointment, despair, or stress within the marriage. The couples who manage to get past those experiences remain in the marriage, mindful of the lessons of the past. In remembering, the individuals concerned readjust their expectations or reframe the relationship to accommodate the new experience or understanding.

An example is when one person has been unfaithful and the other determines that despite the disappointment and hurt, he or she is still committed to the other or the institution of marriage. The betrayed party often withdraws for a time, and the other party does "penance" for a time. At some point the couple, jointly and individually, decide to "remarry." They each can remember enough about the other that is unique, valued, and cherished to propel another round. A new intimacy begins, which may or may not resemble the earlier one. It may never again include aspects of the earlier intimacy, but the satisfaction of relatedness exceeds the pain. Another couple may not survive in identical external circumstances.

The Internal Landscape

What accounts for the decision to recommit after a trauma to the relationship? There is in this family drama a powerful stage director behind the scenes. Each person acts on his or her own stage, which I call the *internal landscape*. After listening to hundreds of stories and thousands of rationalizations, it is the "internal landscape" that determines whether a couple can or cannot survive ruptures in the relationship. It is the "internal landscape" that determines the breaking point for each of us.

Our expectations of what marriage is, and is not, are most variable, yet are vital to an understanding of why divorce is the only acceptable solution for some people whose marriages are in crisis. One person's disappointments may not be another's. But beyond this simplistic statement lies the much more important question. What patterns, intimacies, and lifestyles are prerequisites to a worthwhile marriage in each partner's mind? For some partners, the existence of sexual intimacy is paramount; for others it is negotiable. Financial security may be the bedrock necessity or stability or relatedness. Silence might be the unacceptable, egregious error. Meaningful daily communication may be replaceable to some if everything else is in place.

We all arrive at marriage with a lot of baggage, starting with our own experiences of love. For some people, love can accommodate periods of rejection, disappointment, and distance or periods of unfaithfulness in one's spouse. If a person's parents, or one of them, were unfaithful, he or she is more likely to expect that marriage may involve an unrelated person of the opposite sex from time to time. Love and marriage, in such a person's internal landscape, are not necessarily monogamous at all times. The internal landscape of such a person may in fact define marriage as a commitment to stay together regardless of sexual conduct.

The betrayal or loss of trust in marriage often has little to do with sexual infidelity but arises from a spouse's unreliability at times of crisis or a spouse's persistent disrespect. The ability of the injured party to forgive and approach again in a newly realigned relationship depends upon the ideas of forgiveness, love, and realignment learned in earlier relationships and in their family growing up.

Each of us has uniquely defined thresholds and boundaries. Intimacy, distance, thresholds, and boundaries have everything to do with our family of origin and nothing to do with the person we happened to select as our mate. For many people, the story of why a divorce is, has, or will happen is to be found in a close examination of the interactions of the person's family of origin: How did the family of origin define intimacy, distance, and boundaries? What were the bedrock principles which were sacrosanct in the family? In some families, intimacy and connection are defined by conflict, possessiveness, or intrusion, without regard to the need for the boundaries of other family members. In some families, intimacy is defined as letting the other person alone when he or she is in emotional turmoil. Similarly, distance may be viewed as behaving respectfully and leaving the other with his or her dignity and sense of separate self. The kindest act is considered the lightest touch.

Interpersonal boundaries are not the same from family to family. Each family has its own culture which seems "right" to its members. A marriage requires the spouses to function cross-culturally, which in turn means tolerance for difference and yet a need to forge a working relationship.

In some family cultures, independence of the spouses is admired; in other cultures, interdependency of the spouses is expected. Arguing and fighting may be considered a sign of attention and affection, whereas in other family cultures it is abhorred. Some families speak their feelings directly, while in other families the most serious criticisms can be alluded to only in jest or a pointed tease. Some families place a great deal of importance on "the family," class, or wealth. Other families may not share such sentiments or values.

These sweeping generalizations are not meant to be taken too literally, but they are offered for the purpose of focusing on some of the ways in which all of us have been molded by our past, in conscious and unconscious ways. Definitions of love and its legitimate and illegitimate expression vary enormously, and all of us are more experienced with one form than another. The consequence of familiarity is recognition of love expressed in a melody we know and a sense of deprivation when it is voiced differently. Our interpretation of what love is needs to be checked repeatedly against the reality of the other person's internal landscape, not judged by the rules of our own family's culture.

Careful consideration of how stress, disappointment, betrayal, and loss were dealt with in the family of origin is the best predictor of our own first response to these events. We may prefer to model ourselves after certain family members, but we may unconsciously mimic another in less constructive ways. An understanding of our expectations garnered from our earlier relations are the best indicators of who will, and who will not, reach for aftermarriage as the solution to marital difficulties. A person may elect to copy or reject the model as learned, but being neutral is not an option. Who will make only one exploratory visit to my office and who will return for the full journey depends on each person's character, personality, and internal history, not that of the spouse whose disappointing conduct prompted the visit.

We have internalized models of what a father or mother should be, and how an adult, intimate relationship called marriage should feel. All of this happens without necessarily understanding our own assumptions and expectations. The first place to look when a marriage feels wrong is at these assumptions and expectations. In collecting the history of the client, I always ask about parental wealth (a factor considered by most divorce statutes in the rubric of opportunity to acquire future income and assets) and parental marriages. Often I learn significant information when I delve into the pattern the client considers normal or at least familiar. I do not claim to understand what a "normal" family dynamic is, but I do have enormous respect for its importance in understanding our expectations and comfort zones.

Sometimes a client describes an idyllic childhood and parents who were always considerate of each other, a "Norman Rockwell" home, and I think to myself such a client carries a burden of expectations of harmony and solace in marriage which may be unmatchable given the spouse selected. Other times I am struck by the perversity of the parental conduct, whether it was abuse, self-destructiveness, or the result of a history of mental illness. I wonder whether my client has a genetic predisposition to the same dysfunction or an attraction or hypersensitivity to it in others.

Has the fact that people live so much longer influenced our expectations (and demands) of marriage? We live longer than previous generations and still expect that marriage will last a lifetime. Lengthy marriages, like long-lived lives, have developmental cycles and distinctive stages. When I hear someone say they have outgrown their partner, I wonder whether the couple was ever well matched. With the passage of time, a spouse's internal landscape may no longer be as exciting to explore, and the task of enriching each other is more tiresome. The couples who survive are able to realign their differences with an ease and joy that augment the relationship rather than detract from it. Happily married couples experience realignment not as a burden but as a joint process, an adventure, and an enticing challenge rather than a source of tension, anger, and misunderstanding.

CHAPTER 3

The Classic Marriage Bargain

Most people who are over the age of 40 when they face the break-up of their marriage have a classic marriage bargain: an equal partnership within which the partners perform vital but different roles, sharing the paramount purpose of marriage as understood throughout history and in all religions: procreation. The couple's expectation was to create a family and remain together until death. In contract terms, they had a deal: The wife would stay at home and be the children's primary caregiver while the husband would be the primary provider.

How a person in a classic marriage bargain copes with the process of divorce varies even if the broad pattern of the marriage type is similar. The individual expectations of what will happen as a result of dissolution and what life will be like in after-marriage are critical. The person's emotional capacity to accept the loss of an intact marriage is also significant.

In this chapter and later chapters, the following two couples will illustrate how a similar marital bargain can produce two very disparate divorce experiences and aftermarriage climates. For the four people involved, their journeys to the land of after-marriage, and what they found there, were colored by their expectations, attitudes, emotional fortitude or frailty, and readiness to let go of their marriage.

Mary Ann and Vin

Mary Ann received her divorce papers from Vin's attorney, delivered by a constable at 7:30 A.M. on September 15. I met my new client two days later. Mary Ann arrived half an hour early for her appointment. She was seated on a green sofa in the reception area, next to a woman I later learned was her cousin. Her cousin had driven her to my office because Mary Ann was so unsure about wanting a lawyer that her cousin decided to get her to her appointment, regardless of how pained she felt. The cousin asked if she could come in with Mary Ann. I explained that the attorney-client privilege only applies if the client and attorney are alone, not in the presence of a third party.

"Perhaps it might be easier for Mary Ann to speak to me alone," I suggested, although I thought to myself, "That will be a mixed blessing; I doubt if she will remember anything I say to her, given her state of mind." Having her cousin in the room would provide a retentive third ear and a stabilizing influence, forfeiting absolute confidentiality in favor of a shoulder to lean on. Mary Ann communicated with her eyes to her cousin that she wanted her present, and they both stood and followed me down the long hallway to my office.

Mary Ann began, "I just don't understand how Vin can do this to the boys and me. He really must not understand what he is doing. How could Vin be so selfish when he and the boys mean everything to me?" Vin instigated the separation, and Mary Ann was blindsided by his decision.

They had married when Vin was 21 and Mary Ann 20; their 23rd wedding anniversary was on September 15. Mary Ann and Vin had moved into the Green Valley Condominium Association, which they nicknamed "the Val," less than a year ago. They had sold their large house to downsize a bit after the boys left for college. They had wanted to finance their sons' college education with the profit from the house—or that was the plan she and Vin had talked about. But now Mary Ann was not sure how much of the plan had really happened. She was sure, as she repeatedly pressed the back of her neck where her short hair stopped, that they sold their house on Main Street in the spring. And that not long before or after that, they had signed papers for the purchase of the Val condo for $450,000 and had put down $50,000. But she did not know for sure what had happened to the profit from their home. She had always assumed Vin had used it for their sons' college costs.

I could see Mary Ann trying to swallow her thoughts. Her throat tightened, and she continued. "Vin never, ever talked about divorce, just about how much he needed to travel for business and that he would not be home much this month." She had wanted to believe him but did say that lately, when Vin came home in the early hours of the morning, she had thought she smelled perfume on his shirts before she threw them in the wash. She began to weep and gratefully took the Kleenex her cousin offered her.

Mary Ann's story was a credible report of her experience of the start of her divorce. After all, marriage requires two willing participants, but it only takes one person to decide to divorce. From Vin's perspective (which I heard later but anticipated from Mary Ann's tale), the marriage had been unhappy for some time.

Vin probably told his lawyer his decision to divorce grew very slowly, after much deliberation and consideration; that he thought about leaving for years but did not want to act until his boys were out of the house. He might have told a credible story of a kind, thoughtful father who would never walk out on young children despite how lonely and unfulfilled he felt. He would have described how he avoided many opportunities to be with attractive women, attributing his abstinence to his self-discipline, integrity, and character. He would have said that Mary Ann was a good mother, that he had known she would be from the moment they met. He probably recounted how Mary Ann considered the pay she received as an elementary school teacher "joy-pay."

In fact, Vin carefully selected an attorney he thought would be "gentle." He wanted to be fair to Mary Ann, who had never been anything other than a good mother and homemaker. The "game plan" Vin and his attorney chose was based on Vin's fear that if he tried to talk first to Mary Ann about his wish to divorce, she would feign a plan to commit suicide—or worse, attempt it. She had often said, "If something ever happened to you, I just wouldn't want to live." Vin hated how he felt whenever she said that. He wanted her to be her own person and not be so dependent upon him.

Regardless, he could not discuss with her something that was nonnegotiable: his decision to leave their marriage and to leave for a woman he already knew he wanted. "To pretend to 'discuss' the issue would be cruel," he had said to his attorney, and that was how he felt. His attorney had suggested that Vin warn Mary Ann that she would be receiving papers, but Vin thought that would be equally unkind and pointless.

Henry and Eleanor

All unhappy couples are unhappy in their own way. Henry and Eleanor were unhappy differently from Vin and Mary Ann. They talked about matters in subdued tones, always. As they discussed divorce, their voices were at the same pitch as when they discussed where they would meet at the reception following graduation ceremonies at the college where Henry held the endowed chair in the classics department. They were enormously civilized and pointedly polite in their approach to all feelings—especially fury.

Eleanor had said to Henry, "I think we will both be happier if we are apart. I'm tired of competing with your mistress: the college. I just do not want to hear any more about all the people who are so brilliant and what event you are going to attend next. I just want someone home with me. I want a husband who talks to me, not lectures at me or ignores me. You never talk with me like a best friend—and I mainly go out with you only when it is a performance event at the college. I loathe these functions and am beginning to loathe you for making me go for the sake of appearances and then ignoring me, to say little about the rest of my life. Let's separate. I want to start interviewing divorce lawyers. Why don't you also start, and then we can tell each other whom we have chosen? I want us to do this without any conflict. I know what we own since I take care of the checkbook, and I will prepare a list of our assets. Can you get the latest information on your retirement and pension from the college so that I can have that data when I see whomever I pick?"

Then Eleanor asked, in the same tone of voice, "Do you want any more coffee? I can make another pot. The girls came home at 10:30 last night after they saw a movie. They were so happy to see each other again. I wish they were awake so that you could see them before we all meet at the reception."

"I wish that I could, too," Henry said, as he opened *The New York Times* Arts section, making no comment at all about the divorce plan. "Do you want part of the paper?" Henry noticed that his friend's exhibition was not even mentioned and wondered why.

He was not a particularly introspective man, and he certainly was not sentimental about his private life. On the other hand, he felt enormously attached to the traditions of the college and relished being a part of its history. Eleanor had repeatedly said that the college was his mistress, and Henry essentially agreed. However, he was an excellent provider, was considered a terrific professor, and had excellent taste in all things, particularly men's clothing. Henry believed that his tenured position at the college reflected not only his good fortune but also his scholarly mind and perseverance. He preferred to spend the weekend in his office, at the classics library, or attending a conference. Why shouldn't he do what gave him the most pleasure? How did Eleanor want him to be and why should he change? He knew that at age 62 there was little likelihood that he could change, even if he wanted to—and he did not.

They had enough money, and there were ample accommodations closer to the classics department that might suit him very well, indeed. After all, the house really was quite inconvenient; it had been Eleanor's choice and certainly was her domain. He would never think of asking her and the children to live anywhere else. He rose and said to Eleanor, as he always did upon leaving the house, "Have a good day," adding, "We will meet at the usual place."

In due course, Henry followed his wife's bidding, which is why he came to see me. He was a strikingly handsome man with a head full of jet-black hair highlighted with swaths of white around his temples, a gallant bearing, and a businesslike demeanor. He had several sheets detailing his and his wife's finances—prepared by his wife, he told me. Indeed, Eleanor had efficiently handled their finances for the past 30 years and had invested his earnings very wisely. "Eleanor wants a divorce," Henry told me in his smooth, even-timbered voice. He understood her disappointment and discontent but had no wish to change. He intended to do "whatever is fair," stating that their preference was to proceed as quickly as possible. Henry did not know whom his wife had consulted or retained to represent her, but he said he would let me know as soon as she told him.

As I listened to Henry's matter-of-fact style, admired his organized written material, and sensed his businesslike approach to getting "through" the divorce process with as little fanfare and noise as possible, this case felt very clear. There was no doubt in my mind that representing him would be relatively pleasant and straightforward.

Legal Implications of This Classification

The story as initially told by the client, and as corrected or modified by the story I hear later from his, or her, spouse, does not much resemble the tale I will craft to tell the court. Couples do not usually conceive of their marriage as a contract with implicit and explicit promises, but the court regards the story as a broken bargain, a breached contract. The court is interested in the financial history and circumstances of the parties, not their emotional wounds, no matter how searing. The court needs to hear the factors that are set forth in the applicable divorce statutes, such as the length of the marriage, the age and health of the parties, vocational skills, employability, earned and unearned income, lifestyle, needs of the children, contributions to the marital estate, liabilities, and contribution as homemaker.

Mary Ann, like other people in her circumstance, spoke of betrayal, disloyalty, untrustworthiness, and cheating as she described her disappointment and loss of faith. As her lawyer, I listen to the nature of the marital bargain, the classification of marriage type, the degree of interdependency and reliance that each partner placed in the other. I am also very attentive to the past, present, and future financial and nonfinancial contributions of the parties as all of these issues will matter in court. Mary Ann and Vin and Eleanor and Henry are all involved in some permutation of the classic marriage bargain. This model is most common among divorcing couples in their late forties, fifties, and sixties. The classic model is usually less prevalent in younger marriages.

Even though it takes only one person to breach a marriage, one person cannot change the bargain when divorce occurs. The bargain does not require that they be best friends, or even true intimates; the degree of intimacy they share depends on their connection, their personalities, the pleasure they take in each other's company, and the intellectual and social interests they share.

However, the hard reality is that nobody steps into the provider's role in aftermarriage. The provider's wife performed her tasks: making a home, raising children, and remaining dependent. She has upheld the bargain and will be not only disappointed and hurt, but also ill-equipped to change her role. Because of her childcare responsibilities, the wife will have foregone acquiring the skills of the marketplace. Even after the children leave the nest, she remains dependent. Society at large does not want to be burdened with picking up the pieces, especially if the provider has the financial capacity to continue with his part of the bargain.

In the tug-of-war of the divorce process, the now-estranged wife wants to maintain her lifestyle. The husband wants to pay as little as possible, but he recognizes that his freedom will come at a price. If the children are gone, he may argue that the wife's needs are diminished. The wife will argue that his departure is unfair, as she was willing to perform as she had in the past. Her job has lightened, but the children were bound to grow up, and she has earned the right to a continuation of her lifestyle. Furthermore, she has bypassed opportunities to improve herself, having faith that her husband would not renege on his bargain.

Mary Ann and Vin are the prototypical example of the classic bargain. They were childhood sweethearts and married upon graduation from college at barely 21 years of age. Mary Ann became a skilled elementary school teacher and, in recent years, had opportunities to go into school administration but preferred to remain a "hands-on" teacher. Vin worked in a number of different businesses over their 23-year marriage. Their boys attend Ivy League colleges, a privilege neither parent had. Once the boys left for college and they sold their big house, Vin felt entitled to try his hand at his own business venture, a lifelong dream. He and a friend began a copy business they named Kwik Copy. In short order, Vin and his partner opened several stores. On paper, the business did not show much profit. In the meantime, Vin was relishing his sense of freedom and control over his own destiny. The business allowed Vin to drive a fancy car and indulge in an almost limitless expense account. Vin felt alienated from Mary Ann, and he and his young manager, Jill, with her short skirts and warm, contagious laughter, began spending evenings together. Before long, Vin and Jill became intimate, and Mary Ann learned that she had not just imagined the perfume on Vin's shirts.

Mary Ann finished her most active years as a superb mother of two boys whom she still believed needed their father. She expressed all of her heartbreak and yearning in terms of the boys. She presented herself as attractive, loyal, and courageous in so many ways that her fate felt unjustified to me in terms of her upholding the couple's bargain. However, as she recited the same story over and over again, I did begin to feel sympathy for Vin, who wished to widen his horizons before it was too late.

Movement from marriage to aftermarriage means only that these formerly married people will not live together—not that the provider will not pay support. The obligations of support and maintenance must be performed or the right to nonperformance purchased from the spouse.

Henry seems to have known, intuitively, that the financial obligations of his marriage would never end. Both Henry and Eleanor were prepared to continue to communicate—perhaps no differently and no better than they had before the divorce. Such an attitude is essential to an aftermarriage where parties have children together or have had a long marriage.

Mary Ann was unable to imagine life without Vin. She could not accept that her marriage was not a fixed, firm arrangement. The only thing she wanted to talk to Vin about was what he had done to their family by leaving. Vin would have willingly spoken to her about how to address their continuing parenting responsibilities, but she allowed no such opening.

Mary Ann and Vin entered the divorce process with inflexible attitudes, coupled with unrealizable goals. Unwittingly, they consistently chose paths that maximized their financial and emotional damage. Henry and Eleanor arrived at the process with less ambitious goals as to what a divorce might fix and, therefore, demanded less of the process. They carefully avoided actions that would inflame their relationship and impair their future ability to relate constructively.

CHAPTER 4

The Companion Marriage Bargain

The second category of marriage, the companion marriage bargain, is particularly prevalent among married people in their 20s and 30s. The hallmark of the companion marriage is that the couple are companions for life, best friends, sharing all aspects of their lives. From the beginning of the relationship, implicitly or explicitly, they have agreed to share responsibility for the home, their social life, and childcare if they become parents. The partners hope to create their own paradigm, distinct from a classic marriage bargain, and arrive at a perfect balance of power in the relationship.

The companion marriage is the most elusive and hardest to manage, as it requires that the couple share values (at least as compromised), leadership, control, and power, a difficult assignment at any age. The expectation that it can be done comes not so much from having seen it work, but from younger generations' reaction to the classic model, in which the partners' leadership and control was in separate spheres. Even if economic power resided only with the husband/breadwinner, the wife/homemaker ruled her domain. The emergence of the companion type of marriage can be traced to women's entry into the workplace and the rejection of gender stereotypes. In earlier generations, fewer women worked full-time, and if they worked part-time, it was less likely to be as professionals; fewer men were as involved in homemaking and parenting.

In this marriage bargain, the couple plan to be best friends forever and share everything equally, which requires enormous skill and commitment in negotiating both large and small issues—not just once, but constantly. Consensus and compromise are a daily necessity. In marriages where parties share all spheres, the bargain may fail not so much because one party or the other has changed but because negotiating each and every detail is exhausting. If either party is not a skilled or an equal bargainer, or tires of endlessly negotiating, then the deal fails. The expectations in this model are for complete intimacy in terms of cooperation and intertwining concerns. The couple can only operate if there is harmony of purpose and values and time and space for everything. The model is attractive—even seductive—but the lifestyle is exhausting, particularly when both partners work full-time.

The problems really arise when children arrive, because suddenly there are many competing bosses: work, the children, the home, and the spouse who expects attention from the best friend. When one partner suggests that the paradigm be altered, the other cries foul. "It was our deal to share the decisions!" Neither may really want to continue the strain of sharing, but neither one wants to be told that the sharing is stopping. It was the mantra of their marriage. An offer by one spouse to take over the family finances may cause the other spouse to fume, rather than acknowledge its advantages.

The hurt and disappointment felt upon the break-up of this type of marriage often relates to disappointment in the other person, rather than the intrinsic difficulties with the model—and the pain of sorting out how to share the children. Companion couples often point the finger of fault at their mate for his or her inability to share meaningfully. They express disappointment that their partner has proven to be rigid and overbearing rather than flexible and lighthearted. There is a reluctance to admit how rarely any couple shares each and every value and priority and how stressful reaching accord can be, especially in the midst of active child-rearing responsibilities. The task of continually sharing children from separate residences is far more complex than many companion couples foresee.

Natalie and Martin

Natalie is an efficient, articulate woman in her mid-30s who first came to see me for consultation only to gather information. Even then, I noticed the care and caution with which she approached our meeting. She had spreadsheets of the family income and monthly expenses, retirement accounts, and checking and savings account balances. She had her questions typed out and she checked them off in red ink, taking care not to break her manicured French nails. Natalie is vice president of marketing at a fast-paced computer company. She and Martin have two children: Michael, age 10, and Nicole, age 8. Martin is the parent who is at home most of the time; he works in computers, but as a part-time technical consultant from home, only occasionally going on-site, repairing or monitoring rather than designing or planning programs.

Natalie and Martin have been having a lot of marital tension lately, and each year Natalie feels worse about her choice of a mate. She thinks of Martin as a good and certainly devoted father but describes him as utterly flat, boring, and passive. Maybe her family knew her better than she had known herself 12 years ago, when they wondered whether Martin was the right man for her, not just because they had different religious backgrounds nor even because Martin came from a dysfunctional family. Natalie's brother captured the family's concerns when he said, "Martin and you do not walk the same walk or talk the same talk." She had responded, "We may not talk the same talk, but we hear what the other one has to say." When they first married, Martin had been energetic, thoughtful, and a really effective team player in Natalie's eyes. Of late, they both bristled at the thought of talking about their work with each other, much less any more intimate subject.

Natalie described herself and Martin doing everything together in the first years. They not only worked in the same field, but they also shared friends, hobbies, sports activities, even food shopping. After Martin moved into her one-bedroom condominium, they opened a joint bank account into which they deposited equal amounts to pay their common expenses. If either had more money, the excess was placed in individual accounts. They even bought the same stock(s) with the surplus and prided themselves on the extent to which they were true companions and intimates.

Neither Natalie nor Martin wanted their marriage to be like their parents' marriages. Natalie's parents were very traditional and Martin's were dysfunctional. They had pledged to contribute equally on all fronts, with no separate or unbalanced powers in their relationship.

Since Michael's birth, and even more markedly after Nicole was born, the couple seemed less cozy. Natalie was so pressured with the required travel, deadlines, and fast pace of her job that she had no time to incorporate Martin into every daily task just for the sake of togetherness. Martin now does all the food shopping; they alternate the cooking; and Martin is the parent who tends to help the kids with their school projects and night-time stories. Natalie did say that Martin always has been very diligent about doing his half of the childcare even when the kids were tiny. Over the years he certainly changed as many diapers and went to as many school conferences as she, but "Who is counting?" Natalie asked many questions about custody and how the children's living arrangements are decided in the divorce process. She was very worried that her success at work would be held against her in a settlement.

Their good times had grown fewer and fewer, and their fights had become increasingly rancorous. In their last argument, which was over money, they each threatened the other with divorce. Martin called her a "hard-ass robot." Natalie returned with, "You're as lazy and boring as your father; no wonder your mother left him." What happened to their philosophy of best friends sharing everything?

Natalie suspects that Martin is jealous of her success at work, her high income, and marvelous stock options, and secretly wishes it were he, or at least that they were both "in it" or "out of it" together. She expresses anger and frustration to Martin, saying, "There is only one responsible breadwinner in the family! Why am I the mainstay of the family?" Natalie acknowledged in our meeting that she tends to exaggerate Martin's idleness, but she does worry a lot about finances. She had to finance her own education, clothing, and each and every vacation or treat since she was 16. She ruminates about their compatibility and their future ability to be communicative partners. Everything seems to be going the wrong way.

In a second visit (six months after her initial consultation), Natalie said she was ready to proceed. She felt certain because the arguments were increasingly horrible and the silences that followed were deafening. Even the children asked her, "How come you and Daddy always fight or ignore each other?" Michael had started to act like Martin around her: quiet, sullen, and passive-aggressive. She felt that if she waited any longer to act, the damage to the children would only get worse. She also knew that Martin wouldn't get a real job if she didn't take action. And she felt so lonely and stressed.

As she confessed her hollow, lonely feelings, Natalie looked smart and polished in her turquoise suit, which her shoulder-length blond hair just grazed. I realized that I liked her much more when she confessed her vulnerability and angst about her life and less when she stridently, almost arrogantly, spoke about her success. She was, indeed, a superwoman who had it all, by the standards of professional achievement, marriage, children, and home.

I imagined Martin's story would have points of reference in common with Natalie's, and in time I learned his version. He related that he had been so attracted to Natalie early in their acquaintance. She was everything he wanted and had such a gentle way about her. He had come from a broken home. His mother walked out on his father because, according to her, he couldn't hold a job or lift a finger. Martin was determined to succeed in his personal life, not to be so disaffected and useless at home. He was extremely intelligent, but not fond of taking orders. Consulting suited him, and he was in the midst of negotiating a long-term project for the third time that year. One of these deals would come through. Why did Natalie harp on him so? She never used to nag or question his ambition or competence. Now, with Natalie's hectic schedule and numerous business trips, as well as the demands of the kids' activities, neither he nor Natalie had time for themselves, much less for each other.

Martin wants Natalie to food shop with him and the kids; he wants her to slow down and join the family. He wants to talk with Natalie about which lawnmower to buy, and buy it together. He doesn't want a divorce, and he would do just about anything to avoid it. He loves the children and wishes they could go back to the kindly cooperation of their early days, when they all sat in the kitchen baking muffins and playing cards while the stove emitted its magical smell. But Natalie has stubbornly refused to consider working on their marriage. She wants only to talk to him through lawyers. I hope to educate Natalie about how important her continued direct communication with her husband is, even if they are divorcing. Talking only through lawyers is not in her interest or her children's. She and Martin have many years of parenting to do together, and their children will need both of them fully involved and able to communicate.

Both Natalie and Martin want to stay with the children in the house. Each parent is highly fit, on both legal grounds and, more importantly, in each other's eyes. Natalie knows that the kids adore Martin; she also knows that he has a lot of patience and less of a temper than she has. But Natalie is financially secure, and the same may not be true of Martin. As talented as he is, she doesn't think he can conform to an office setting, even if he is a pied piper with the children.

The Children's Best Interests

Parenting issues will dominate Natalie and Martin's case, and with the increased role of men in the raising of children, the issue of how to share the children is increasingly difficult to resolve. The traditional custody arrangement of one parent as primary and the other as visiting is less appropriate to the companion marital bargain than the classic marriage bargain. The older divisions by gender have ceased, and with that has come greater confusion about how best to share children who are equally bonded to and accustomed to daily care from both parents.

The court relies on the principle of the "best interests of the children" for the solution. The lawyers have the task of interpreting their client's circumstances with this in mind. The court measures "best interests" in terms of stability and continuity of care, school, home life, and extended family. A parent's financial resources are usually not a paramount factor. The outcome will be much more influenced by which parent will allow the other ready access to the children.

Natalie's concern that she may not be awarded custody of the children is realistic, since both parents have been very present in the children's lives. Natalie fears Martin may even be able to show a greater bond with the children. However, if she were to remain in the home, she would not need any financial subsidy from Martin, and the children would have continuity of lifestyle. Natalie would also promise not to withhold the kids from Martin, which she could amply demonstrate: her clear desire to rely on Martin for childcare and her acknowledgement of his beneficial role in their lives would be significant factors in her favor.

Martin may argue that a reversal of the traditional gender roles has occurred in their marriage: He is the stay-at-home house-husband who has been the mainstay for the home and the children, and Natalie should pay him child support so that he can remain in that role. Many judges (particularly male) take the view, expressed or not, that the husband's time at home is temporary, really only happening because some professional event in his life has yet to happen. Natalie's attorney might emphasize that Martin is on the brink of several work deals, that his time at home will be short-lived, and the sharing of the children should not be arranged around this temporary situation. Martin's attorney would deny this spin and demonstrate that the recent parenting patterns point to his client as the primary one. Continuity in the children's care is of paramount importance.

Natalie and Martin's marital bargain may be alluded to in arguments about financial and child-related issues, because it provides the context for the expectations they had for their marriage. Even if Martin is less financially successful than Natalie, the expectation was that they would share equally the household maintenance and child-related care and costs. Neither party expected the other to support him or her, unlike the classic marriage bargain. Furthermore, Natalie and Martin are relatively young, only in their 30s. They have a lifetime of earning potential ahead, and they may each marry again.

How Natalie and Martin proceed toward aftermarriage is critical to their future ability to communicate. Throughout the divorce process, Natalie needs to be counseled to remember that, regardless of her desire for distance, she will be inextricably linked to Martin for years to come because of the children. Although they will no longer live together or be "best friends," Natalie and Martin will have to communicate with each other constantly about the children, their needs, their schedules, and the parents' own work/vacation plans as they may impact upon the children. The skills of co-parenting, so necessary in their model of marriage, are even more necessary in aftermarriage.

CHAPTER 5

The Protectorate Marriage Bargain

In the protectorate marriage bargain, one party agrees to provide for and protect the other. The marriage is usually childless and of longer duration than the failed affair/childless, short marriage. If you put it in the stark terms of a contract, the deal is that, in exchange for safety and material comfort, the protected party agrees to admire and adore his, or her, protector, with no power or control over any domain. An example would be the wealthy older man with the young trophy wife; the wealthy older woman with the younger consort is another.

The adored person is typically the more emotionally expressive partner, and it is his, or her, burden to provide a happy emotional climate; should he, or she, fail to feed the ego and pleasure of the protector, the marriage may flounder. Although spouses are described as equal partners in marriage, the protectorate bargain was formed because opposites attract. The couple may never have consciously discussed their power imbalance during the courting stage, unless the wealthier spouse demanded a prenuptial agreement in order to protect assets. During an ongoing protectorate, few couples reorganize their power dynamics.

Upon divorce, the protected spouse often has unrealistic expectations of the value of his or her contribution to the marriage. Mid-length protectorate marriages without children provide little protection to a dependent spouse. Unlike a long-term classic marriage, alimony awarded in protectorate marriages, often termed rehabilitative alimony, is of short duration. Assets are not equally shared, as that would be inequitable in light of the disparity of the spouse's original financial circumstances. At best, a dependent, protected spouse can only hope to receive a continuation of her marital lifestyle for a relatively brief period of time.

The protected spouse may be accustomed to the lifestyle and expect it to continue into the future, but the State's interest in ensuring continuity of lifestyle for the sake of children is absent. A dependent spouse ought not be left destitute, as that could burden State welfare, but short of that, a provider will not be made to endlessly provide a luxurious lifestyle. If the protected party seeks the divorce, he or she may feel less entitled to support and less surprised by its termination. On the other hand, if the protected party views himself or herself as the victim of the wealthier spouse's desire to end the marriage, the financial outcome may seem unduly harsh.

Although the story that follows is in this category of marital bargains, it has an additional dimension beyond the uneven nature of the charitable or protectorate marriage.

Bettina and Mark

As Bettina left her art studio in her recently gentrified city neighborhood, she thought about her conversation with Mark in the car the night before. He had looked at her differently; she felt it in her bones. He had that glint of impatience in his eyes and that clipped speech she hated. He just was not *there* in some way, and she felt as if he resented being there, with no escape from her. It was not so much what he said, it was how he said it: "I just don't think it's in my heart to try any more fertility tests." She was now

41, and they had been trying for five years. He was right, she knew, but it still hurt to give up trying to have a baby. Mark had always said that, given his Italian background, a marriage without children was not a marriage. Bettina was scared that Mark would leave her. In fact, she knew he would; it was only a matter of time.

She dreaded this. As she approached their "love nest," she felt so sad. Their Victorian house was a symbol of her disappointment, her beautiful substitute cradle. She had perfectly restored it with hours of sweat equity and a keen eye for detail. Bettina was a somewhat talented and very beautiful painter when they met. She worked on her painting throughout their 10-year marriage, while restoring the house for the past four. Although her body had ultimately let them down, she had taken care of her appearance: her pure skin; svelte, curvaceous figure; and curly, auburn hair.

But what difference did it make? What mattered was that Dr. G. had told her he doubted she could ever bear children, and that was unacceptable to Mark. Bettina felt horribly unloved, and Mark did little to reassure her. She tried to ignore her fears, her feelings of rejection and inadequacy, and waited to see if Mark would take the first step out of their marriage.

Bettina did not have long to wait. Mark was already shopping for a lawyer. He had gotten the name of his friend Ben's lawyer; his work as a physician consumed so much of his day that setting aside time to meet several lawyers was impossible, and he was satisfied with Ben's lawyer's approach, who suggested that the parties try to reach an amicable resolution, since the only major asset of the marriage was the house. Mark did not own his own medical practice; he was an employee of a managed-care corporation and had earned his medical license before they married. He decided to tell Bettina that she should find counsel to represent her as soon as possible. The house's value had skyrocketed since its purchase four years ago, and he would share the profits with her equally, even though he had paid the down payment and the costs of renovation and maintenance.

Bettina and I met on a cold, wintry morning. She was like a bird with a broken wing, and her sense of despair and fear were palpable as she entered my office. I could anticipate that her painful story would not fare well in court. There were no children to protect, which would have prevented the court from ordering a sale of the home. Bettina could expect to receive a share of the profit from the house sale and some level of temporary support, but the question would be for how long and at what level. She had been an impoverished artist before her marriage and would be again in the land of aftermarriage unless she changed careers. The court might well impute to her a reasonable amount of earned income in light of her age, health, and education.

Bettina's choice to spend her time dabbling as an artist was a luxury that Mark may have been willing to support when married, but not one that the court would impose on him afterward. Her dependency may have been entrenched, but it had not been created by Mark. His charitable attitude toward her self-indulgent lifestyle had provided a decade of relief, but neither Mark nor society had reaped a tangible reward from it, other than renovations to the house. I advised Bettina that her strongest weapon was to appeal to Mark's sense of compassion and approach the separation and divorce with as much honey and as little vinegar as possible. Mark's feelings of guilt were Bettina's best ally, not her claim of entitlement to permanent support.

The legal attitude toward the protectorate marital bargain is that the bargain may have been a contract in form, but in substance, the support and protection were essentially a gift from one party to the other. Once the parties separate, that lifestyle should be curtailed as rapidly as possible. To the extent feasible, the recipient should not benefit beyond the charity given voluntarily: Any claim of dependency will be viewed with a jaundiced eye. Failure to actualize the primary purpose of marriage (in this case, childbirth), even when seriously pursued, will affect the outcome upon dissolution. The party who provided support, with little tangible reward, ought to be allowed to relinquish that role. Mark agreed to protect Bettina, but he had an undeniable yearning to have children. He could not change his feelings. His feelings were not against Bettina even though his decision caused Bettina's pain and abandonment.

The constant process of examining our life choices is indigenous to the human spirit, to varying degrees at different stages. The implicit imbalances of the protectorate marriage make it especially prone to alterations in the bargain as individuals evolve and change. Although in this case it is Mark, the provider, who wants to dissolve the marital agreement, in some cases the dependent party may be the one desiring a change. He or she may have struck the original marriage bargain because of a need to run away from a dysfunctional family or to have a life on his or her own. But such individuals may grow and become dissatisfied with their dependence and lack of power in a protectorate marriage, and instability will follow. Sometimes the protector, in mid-life crisis, senses the passage of time and recalculates the costs of his (or her) generosity. Either way, altering the marital bargain—and staying married—may or may not be possible.

CHAPTER 6

The Complex Marriage Bargain

The complex marital bargain includes a significant person or group of people (parents or extended family) with a bearing on the marriage and its survival. This marriage type also includes all remarriages, which are complex by definition, particularly where there is not only an ex-spouse but also children from a prior marriage.

The complex marital bargain can take many forms. Its hallmark is that the couple knows that they are not exclusively, emotionally interdependent; one or maybe both members of the couple are intimately connected with someone outside of the partnership. Such a person may be an ex-spouse, a close friend, a parent or sibling, or one's whole family of origin. Because of these emotional attachments or support, crucial to one or both spouses' well-being, the marriage works, until something happens that causes the three-legged stool to wobble. Sometimes an argument, departure, or death causes the marriage bargain to become unstable. Sometimes the marriage survives without it, or a substitute is found.

In remarriages with children from a prior marriage, the ex-spouse is invariably one of the complex partners, along with the children. An ex-spouse and children are substantial presences to be reckoned with, and the newcomer to the aftermarriage family may find it difficult to locate a comfortable perch. She, or he, may resent that the former spouse has compartments of aftermarriage life that are off-limits. Such complex marriages, integrated as they are with someone else's *aftermarriage,* provide the clearest evidence of how important it is to keep aftermarriage in mind when going through the divorce process: If you hope to one day enjoy a successful marriage after this one, make sure you end this one on constructive terms.

In contract language, the nature of this marriage's bargain is that neither party will jostle to displace the "extra" and will accept the existence of the extra. In the story that follows, the complexity stems from the wife's deep attachment to her family.

Zack and Ginny

Zack and Ginny each retained counsel within a year of Ginny's parents' death in a car crash. Zack and Ginny had four lovely, grown children, a beautiful home in the suburbs, no financial worries, and excellent health. Ginny had had an intense and, from Zack's perspective, unhealthy and suffocating relationship with her parents and her twin sister. Every Sunday the extended family ate together at Zack and Ginny's home, since they had the most spacious and gracious setting for the clan gatherings. Zack initially enjoyed these gatherings, as his own family had never been close. But Ginny's family's form of togetherness became less and less comfortable for him. Zack was not a clan man, and it irked him that Ginny would not consider any event or vacation with him alone or even with just the two of them and their children.

After the sudden death of Ginny's parents, the marriage floundered. Ginny was inconsolable, disoriented, and distant. Zack understood her grief, but he felt abandoned. They saw a marriage counselor, but nothing really changed. They just carried on, waiting for relief from the melancholy. All their friends were splitting, and they each wondered if time apart might help their situation. They discussed the possibility in counseling and agreed to separate.

They hired attorneys, but they promised that they would mediate and not litigate, even if they were advised to do so. I met Ginny on this basis. I was retained to coach her through the mediation process only, and I said that I would serve in that role only on the condition that each of us would be free to withdraw if the process or the result proved unacceptable.

Complex marital bargains can take many other forms. The story of Duncan, his new wife and his ex-wife illustrates a few complexities that cause previously married spouses, with children from a prior marriage, to seek legal advice long after divorce. Their story will not be carried forward into other chapters as they have completed the divorce process, unlike Ginny and Zack.

Duncan, Cathy, and Kit

Duncan had been married to Kit, a college sweetheart. They had three children, now aged 23, 21, and 9. Duncan had strayed on a regular basis, but his affair with Cathy, a co-worker, became more than a passing fling. Eventually, he divorced Kit in order to marry Cathy. Kit and Duncan had a vituperative divorce with no regard for how their aftermarriage would be.

All of Kit's pent-up anger, accumulated over the years of infidelity, came bursting out during the separation and divorce. Kit hated Duncan and herself for not having been more self-protective during their marriage. She had assumed that if she turned a blind eye to Duncan's many affairs, he would keep up his end of the bargain and remain married to her. Afterward, she felt betrayed, discarded, and replaced, and had an unconscious agenda to alienate the children from their father.

Duncan knew he had caused the break-up but reasoned that he was tired of living a lie, that his marriage to Kit was a sham. He and Cathy shared so many interests and were so companionable. He imagined that they could have the marriage he had always hoped for: the equal, "best friend" marriage available to enlightened, modern men and women. Unlike Kit, who nagged and bored him, Cathy was smart, pretty, and fun to be with, vibrant and positive about life and the future. Duncan assumed that Kit would come to accept the appropriateness of their marriage ending. She deserved to be well loved and not just live with a half-committed husband who had affairs. He thought that if he was generous in the settlement, he could terminate the marriage without a hassle.

However, after Duncan and Cathy married, the issues with Kit and the children did not settle down. Kit remained resentful and never made anything easy or smooth for Duncan and Cathy. Kit felt that she alone deserved the children's loyalty and wanted the children to see Duncan only if and when he was alone. She spoke of the children needing protection from the confusion of the situation, and how difficult it was for them to accept Cathy as a stepmother, given how Cathy had entered their lives.

Had anyone asked the children how they felt, they would have said that their mother was being harsh with their father, but they respected how she felt. The older two children, a daughter and son, wished keenly to protect their mother from further hurt. Kit let the children know how fragile she was in subtle and not-so-subtle ways. When Duncan offered the children "goodies," such as a vacation to the Bahamas or a new computer, Kit only knew that she was never offered a week in the sun when she and Duncan were together. Kit's bitterness was her emotional reality and a contaminating force in Duncan's relationship with his children and his idealized remarriage.

I became familiar with this complex remarriage when Duncan sought my counsel in connection with a modification of his child-support order after the emancipation of the two older children. They had finished college, and only one unemancipated child remained at home with Kit. Duncan believed that Kit no longer needed as much child support and that she could now return to work full-time as a nurse, especially since Cathy had contributed funds to assist with college costs and expenses. That had not really been fair to Cathy, and she now wanted less money going to his first family, in case they wanted children in the future. Duncan also hoped that if he and Kit had another go-round in court, Kit might rethink her attitude toward his place in the children's lives.

I could not give Duncan much comfort. On the support questions he raised, the relevant questions were, "What were the parties' financial situations at the time of the divorce hearing, what are they today, and has there been a substantial change of circumstances, warranting a modification?" Courts are very reluctant to redo any earlier decision unless such conditions are met.

Duncan's income had grown handsomely since his divorce from Kit. Cathy was employed and their combined incomes were significantly greater than Duncan's earnings at the time of his divorce hearing. Contrary to Duncan's logic, I remarked on his improved situation. Kit's part-time job and her remuneration were unchanged. While one child costs less than three, child support does not get reduced equally as each child becomes independent. Child support varies only marginally upon each child's emancipation. The lion's share of the child-support order has the purpose of addressing the inequality of incomes in the two households, not the number of children to be supported. I doubted that he would be entitled to any reduction in the amount of child support as the ratio of his gross income to his former wife's had probably grown more disparate over the years. Duncan's income had risen far faster than his ex-wife's, and her housing and living expenses were unlikely to be substantially lower than they had been at the time of their divorce, despite the emancipation of the two older children.

As for giving Duncan any assurance that more litigation would alleviate his troubles with Kit, I disappointed him greatly. Not only would he probably not win his request to reduce his child support, he risked Kit's requesting to *increase* the amount! He could not make Kit rethink her bitterness by causing her further losses. The quality of his aftermarriage with Kit would be improved, if at all, by showing his appreciation of her and her past and present mothering. If he volunteered to contribute more to her household, she might soften, but withdrawing funds could only increase her bitterness and her emotional bankruptcy.

I suggested that he consider offering to pay for postdivorce family therapy for the youngest child, Kit, and himself. If a therapist intervened in the aftermarriage dynamics, it might be possible to salvage his relationship with the youngest child. At the time of his consultation with me, Duncan admitted that he had not seen the nine-year-old for nearly a month—Kit always had excuses for not helping to arrange a visit.

I suggested to Duncan that if his offer to pay for family counseling fell on deaf ears, then and only then might he consider a modification action, focused on enforcing therapeutic intervention and implementing visitation rights with the youngest child. The older, emancipated children could not be "made" to do anything. He and they would have to find their own relationship. I urged him to attempt regular contact with all the children: Call, write, send presents every holiday and birthday, regardless of whether they responded. Given the hurt and sense of rejection their mother and they had internalized, it was important that they knew that they were neither disposable nor forgotten, even if he had only one-way communication with them for a very long time before they acknowledged him. Duncan agreed to try my approach, or so he said in my office. We agreed that we would stay in touch and that he would give me a call in a month.

Duncan's remarriage to Cathy, following his stormy divorce from Kit, had little chance of being anything but fraught with difficulties. His expectations of shedding his first marriage and having a clean start with his second were unrealistic. His new wife thought that she and her husband had an exclusive partnership, that her new husband could deliver on his promise that they would have nothing to do with his past life. Cathy was also uninformed of the meaning of a complex marital bargain.

Duncan might have handled matters more carefully with his first family had he had a better understanding of his new marriage and taken a more realistic view of divorce from a marriage with children. However, this scenario is not easy even under the best of circumstances.

Preparing for Aftermarriage

Rushing headlong toward divorce sidesteps the necessary emotional homework to prepare for aftermarriage. The ideal is to wait until both parties are ready to let go. Kit and Duncan needed time and a forum in which to understand the flaws in their own marital bargain and the impossibility (or unwillingness) of realignment within it.

How the couple will behave toward each other after the day in court needs to be addressed. How do they want to behave? How *will* they behave, considering their relationship at the time of the divorce? Whenever and wherever possible, divorcing couples should be urged to engage in "disentanglement" counseling for the purpose of understanding why their marriage has proven disappointing to one, or both, people and to discuss and prepare for a new relationship in aftermarriage. Aftermarriage requires realignment because of the new physical arrangement of sharing children in the context of two homes. In counseling, couples have an opportunity to forge a post-divorce marital construct and discuss the possibility of remarriage after a first marriage with children.

The task of harmonizing or aligning ideas about how couples should behave in aftermarriage is far more challenging than seeking accord in an intact marriage. The feelings of love and goodwill that once made discussion and compromise easier may be completely gone. And yet the stakes are just as high.

The couples we have looked at, Mary Ann and Vin, Eleanor and Henry (classic marriage couples); Natalie and Martin (companion marriage couple); Bettina and Mark (protectorate marriage couple); and Ginny and Zack, Kit and Duncan (complex marriage couples), all failed somehow to successfully adapt to each other's expectations of marriage or change in their own marital construct. In the next chapter, the five types of marital bargains will be set in the broader context of "the box of reasonable settlement." The facts of each divorce case dictate the boundaries of the box, but not all divorcing couples choose to settle within those boundaries.

CHAPTER 7

The Box of Reasonable Settlement

There is a box of reasonable settlement for every case. Pretending that the outcome of a divorce is totally unknowable or completely unpredictable is an extreme position. In most cases, the result—at least in broad-brush terms—is foreseeable to experienced attorneys, mediators, and judges. Just as weather forecasters may not always be able to predict every detail of the day to come, they know the seasonal variations and expectations, the temperature range, and the likelihood of precipitation. We may scoff at their abilities, but we do continue to listen and rely on their speculations because much of the time they are accurate.

A couple's marital bargain, together with relevant financial and employment information (past circumstances, present circumstances, and future circumstances) is sufficient information to make a prediction of the likely contours of the box of reasonable settlement. There are patterns to divorce resolutions. The five types of marriage—the classic marriage, the companion marriage, the protectorate marriage, the complex marriage, and the childless/short marriage—are categories, like seasons, which dictate certain predictable results.

Divorcing people need to be educated about the existence and contours of their relevant box of reasonable settlement. Often a person does not know that an asset is subject to division upon divorce. Pensions and other retirement benefits are examples, as are future interests in trusts, royalties, and unvested stock options. Inherited and/or gifted property may (or may not) be marital property, depending upon where the divorce occurs.

The two primary components of every divorce are the division of assets and the level of ongoing support, if any. Support includes child support and spousal support. The length of the marriage and the nature of the original marriage bargain, as maintained or altered by circumstances, set the stage for reasonable resolution of any divorce.

The box of reasonable settlement may have fuzzy margins, but its general shape is obvious once the category of marriage is labeled and the salient facts known. The fuzzy margins mean that there is a narrow range of reasonable negotiation between able attorneys, if both attorneys are working with the same set of facts. Of course, the facts may not be agreed upon, and that may be the genuine source of the problem in resolving a divorce.

The statistics that follow are based on my experience and that of many experienced matrimonial attorneys in my state. To the extent that states may vary in their traditions, the percentages may be too high or too low. But the essential concept that for every case there exists a box of reasonable settlement remains constant.

Reasonable Box in Childless, Short Marriages

When and if possible, the box of reasonable settlement in a childless, short marriage of less than five years leaves the parties with at least as much as they entered with in terms of assets. Neither party will have to pay support for the other in most instances, unless there is an enormous disparity in income and assets. If so, there may be a minor adjustment, but by no means equal, or necessarily even 65/35. This is especially true if the people are relatively young. The goal is simply to leave each as they would have been had there been no marriage. That outcome is the primary agenda of the box of reasonable settlement in a childless, short marriage.

Reasonable Box in Classic Marriages

Classic marriage bargains of 15 years or more dictate that all marital assets and liabilities be divided equitably, which 90 percent of the time means equally. If the parties are enormously wealthy, exact parity may not occur. "Equitable" may mean something less, or more, than 50 percent if one asset is impossible to divide now, or in the future, or if one spouse will, for example, inherit substantial property in the very near and certain future. Deviation from the norm of equality is very rare, and less than 2 percent of all long marriages terminate with one party receiving greater than 65 percent of the assets.

The amount and duration of spousal support in a classic marriage bargain divorce case varies according to whether the case has been brought in a state where alimony (spousal support) is liberally granted and whether the state follows community property laws wherein property owned by a spouse prior to marriage is not subject to division upon divorce, or equitable distribution laws. Regardless, experienced professionals will know the patterns of resolution, so anyone in a classic marriage can expect an outcome in accord with the way these kinds of cases are resolved in their state.

The law of marriage has bound the parties to "maintain and support" each other. The words "for better or for worse, in sickness and health" would be hollow if they could be disregarded. The person who wants to leave the marriage may do so, but not without sharing the fruits of the union with the person who has made professional sacrifices or never developed a career in order to hold up the marriage bargain. If the couple only had one source of income during the intact marriage, then a reasonable box of settlement should not be crafted in reliance on two sources of support. How often one hears that the unemployed partner ought to go out and get a job now that the other spouse wants to depart! People who approach divorce as a time to change all the habits and patterns of marriage will find themselves disappointed.

The level of support of children usually varies no more than 10 percent from the level recommended in the child support guidelines which exist in all states in the United States by act, statute, regulation, or guideline. The amount (or level) of child support varies from one state to another as well as the method of its calculation. The level of child support is very predictable when parties have a traditional marriage. Only if the family provider's earned (and/or unearned) income exceeds the child support guideline ceiling is the level of child support not readily discernable. Income above the child support guideline ceiling may be labeled support of the wife. The purpose of combining child support and support of the wife (alimony) in divorces of wealthier couples is to minimize federal and state income taxes. As alimony is deductible from gross income of the payor and includible in the gross income of the recipient, it is often wise to incorporate this benefit into the structure of the support package. The allocation of support as between alimony and child support is a "fuzzy" but an important aspect of the box of reasonable settlement. The award (amount and duration) of alimony may vary greatly from state to state, as previously mentioned. Yet there are predictable conventions based on the relevant statutes in each state which may lend guidance to the "fuzzy" contours of the box.

The law of support and maintenance is not eliminated by the legal fiction of divorce. The provider is obligated to support and maintain his, or her, spouse in aftermarriage as in marriage. Neither the most able lawyer nor the fairest judge can make this myth a financial reality. No Houdini magic can make the same income stream (or streams) support two homes as comfortably as one because two homes invariably are more costly than one. The unavoidable shortfall caused by increased expenses must be allocated between the spouses, and that inevitably requires accommodation by all concerned.

Sexual affairs or long-term dalliances by either party do not alter the basic concept of support and maintenance of a spouse. The law regarding support of one's spouse has evolved in this matter due to society's interest in ensuring that the provider, not the government, is tagged with the obligation of support.

Reasonable Box in Companion Marriages

In companion marriages assets are divided equitably, usually meaning 50/50, if the parties have been married for more than five years and entered the marriage with approximately the same assets. If the companion couple received gifts or inheritances during the course of their companion marriage, such assets may not be split equally. But again, there are very few reasonable settlements that leave spouses with a disparity of assets greater than 65/35, regardless of the source of assets. This generalization may be less true in states that are governed by community property laws (where all property owned by a spouse prior to marriage is outside of the marital pot and, therefore, not subject to division upon divorce).

The central issue upon divorce in most companion marriages is the sharing of the children and the application of the child support guidelines to the parties' child-sharing arrangements. The child support guidelines contemplate a traditional, classic marriage arrangement. The assumption of most child support guideline charts is that there is a primary home for the children and a parent who resides elsewhere and therefore sees the children less than two—or two and a half—days a week.

In many companion marriages, the parents want to continue their philosophy of sharing the rearing of the children far more equally than that contemplated in a traditional arrangement. Hence the contours of the reasonable box of settlement hinge on actual child-sharing patterns and whether or not a nontraditional child support arrangement is appropriate. The reasonable box of settlement where parties truly share the care of the children equally, or almost equally, is a reduction of child support, if any, paid by one spouse to the other, provided the parties have comparable incomes. If the parents do, in fact, earn substantially the same income (or within 15 percent of each other), and the children spend at least three days a week with each parent, then no traditional child support payment may be an appropriate resolution. In lieu of traditional child support, the *companion* couple may agree to an equal sharing of all the direct expenses of the children (such as day care costs, clothes, lessons, camp, and extraordinary medical and dental expenses).

As both parents are employed in the companion marital bargain, alimony (support of a spouse) is seldom awarded in a marriage bargain of this kind.

Reasonable Box in Protectorate Marriages

The box of reasonable settlement in protectorate marriage bargains resembles the classic marriage in that one party will be obligated to pay support to the other. The duration of the support will be keyed into the length of the protectorate arrangement. If the marriage has been longer than five years but less than fifteen, the weaker spouse will be likely to receive alimony for a period of time, less than the length of the marriage and more than a year or two. The recipient of the protector's largesse will need a reasonable amount of time to regain her, or his, footing. As there are no children and, therefore, the primary business of marriage was not fulfilled, the duration of alimony will be less than the length of the marriage and often not more than half of its duration. The assets in a protectorate marriage may not be split equally, especially if one party came in with a great deal more money than the other. And this is especially true in second marriages where the protector may have children from a prior marriage to protect ahead of a second wife. In conflict with this policy is the claim of the weaker spouse to receive some semblance of parity and certainly not be left disadvantaged by the union. Even if a spouse came with no assets to such a marriage, a fair and reasonable resolution is unlikely to suggest that such a spouse leave the marriage with no assets, particularly if contrasted with a very wealthy former partner. Again, the statistic of a division which is no more lopsided than 65/35 should be kept in mind.

A suggestion that all assets remain with one party in a protectorate marriage is not within the box of reasonable settlement. And the suggestion that all assets be split 50-50 in this type of marriage is equally unreasonable.

Reasonable Box in Complex Marital Marriages

Anticipating the box of reasonable settlement in a complex marital bargain may involve the same principles as in a classic marriage if the complexity is confined to the existence of a third person, who did not share in the economic benefits of the marriage. However, if the marriage involved funds diverted away from the marital enterprise, the reasonable resolution may be complex. Generalizing this kind of box of reasonable settlement is difficult as such a box is very fact specific. The box may have to encompass the interests of children from a prior marriage or support obligations to a former spouse. However, the burden of persuading a court to divide the assets less than equally is always on the party asserting such an outcome. And again, the likelihood of inequality exceeding 65/35 is very slim.

No Ripeness to Settle: The Case of Mary Ann

The foregoing generalizations assume that both husband and wife desire a reasonable resolution of the financial aspects of their disentanglement, as defined by the conventions of past, similar cases. Unfortunately, not all people willingly and agreeably follow the most likely scenario. There must be a ripeness to settle amicably and readily; without that ripeness, the quality of the offer of settlement is irrelevant.

People who are emotionally unable to allow the marriage to change are the most difficult to represent in a divorce. Mary Ann was constitutionally unable to recognize, other than sporadically and intellectually only, that her physical connectedness with Vin required his ongoing willingness. During the entire three-year divorce process, she refused to accept the end of her intact marriage or to take steps toward protecting herself financially from further disaster by accepting Vin's reasonable offer of settlement. Vin, while not swift in complying with discovery, ultimately had portrayed his assets and income sufficiently to craft a settlement. However, there was no deal, no matter how favorable, that could compensate Mary Ann for her losses, and money did not assuage her feelings of hopelessness, despair, and pain. The dissolution of her marriage was a travesty, and she would not condone Vin's outrageously unfair conduct for her own sake and that of the boys.

When I met with Mary Ann and her cousin at our initial conference, I consciously did not paint the rosiest picture of the possible financial outcome of her case. I try never to promise more than I think can realistically be obtained. It is a mistake to create unrealistic expectations on the part of the client. I always would rather err by "hanging black crepe" and then come out looking "golden" for managing a better outcome. Perhaps this strategy could be viewed as manipulative, but it leaves my reputation more intact than had I obtained the client by promising the moon. I would caution any client against picking an attorney based on what he or she wants to get, only on what the attorney promises to do in order to maximize the chances of success. Mary Ann had acted as if she understood that I would be powerless to prevent Vin from obtaining a divorce. Mary Ann's cousin understood that one party can steam-roll a result, even if not speedily. I knew that Mary Ann was distraught at our first meeting because she so obviously had been unprepared for Vin's declaration of independence, and that she was not ready to proceed. What I did not realize was that she would be unable to accept its reality even with the passage of time. I thought she would be open to an agreement if a reasonable one were offered by the time the discovery process was completed.

Mary Ann's unmanaged, relentless, and intransigent despair propelled her to make facts of her feelings. She could not be persuaded to accept a better deal than would be offered in a court judgment. She had to have her day in court, a day of protest and an opportunity to translate her internal emotional pain into an objective fact. Mary Ann could not compel Vin to remain with her and the boys, but she could make him go to trial, and that was a form of power in the relationship. She would affect their lives destructively by insisting that a trial occur at great legal expense for a financial outcome that was less favorable to her than Vin's pretrial offer of settlement.

Character was destiny. The way in which Mary Ann traveled to the land of aftermarriage had nothing to do with the legal complexity of the case but had everything to do with her ripeness to let go and her compulsion to make her feelings into facts.

By the time the parties reached trial, the marital pot had been reduced by large legal bills and lower business profits than anticipated. Vin was no longer willing to gamble on the success of his new business venture and assure Mary Ann that he would maintain her marital lifestyle, even if doing so would have squeezed him mercilessly. With time, his guilt feelings were abating. Vin had experienced that he could not carry the costs of two homes as comfortably as one; the financial stresses of divorce had cascaded down upon the parties, and he questioned his own divorce expectations.

In contrast to Mary Ann, Henry, the husband in the other classic marriage bargain had also not wanted the divorce originally. His wife, Eleanor, had wanted the separation. Henry was opposed to it but practical and enough of a businessman to consider the cost-benefit of each course of action. Early in the case, he asked for the parameters of a reasonable settlement and accepted the high cost of a long-term marriage with only a gentle grunt.

The differences between these two classic marriage cases lie less in the nature of the appropriate box of reasonable resolution than in the readiness of the parties to emotionally disentangle and live within those strictures. Unquestionably, disentangling was smoother for Henry and Eleanor because there was more money to go around, less of a diminution in lifestyle, and less of an adjustment. Also, they may each have been living emotionally separate lives for years already. Mary Ann was still firmly tied to the idea, if not the reality, of her marriage. Nevertheless, the legal principles governing the outcomes were identical.

Feelings from Outside the Box

Some couples may agree on a settlement that is outside the conventional box, frequently to their own long-term detriment. Such agreements usually happen as a result of the feelings of one, or both, spouses, whether those feelings are guilt, anger, or fear.

Guilt is a powerful, often unacknowledged, force in any divorce, driving the conduct of both husbands and wives. Men seeking divorce are motivated to offer more than they might have because of the concern that they have bankrupted their wives emotionally. Women who initiate divorce all too often express their guilt about an affair by not feeling entitled to continue parenting in the same capacity, or are reluctant to ask for their share of the assets. Despite divorce laws' tolerance toward sexual infidelity, people carry an unacknowledged belief that sexual misconduct should be considered.

Guilt can also be felt for other reasons. Mark, Bettina's husband in their protectorate marriage, was not sure why he could not accept life without children of his own or accept Bettina as she was. He felt bad because he did care for her; maybe not enough or in the right ways, but he did feel guilty and compassionate. I could feel the presence of this silent "third party" in the settlement discussion. Bettina had asked to postpone our four-way meeting (the couple and their attorneys) for two weeks so she could be stronger in Mark's presence. Mark was a pleasant-looking person, stockier than I had anticipated and much shyer. With shyness and shame, he looked across the table and said to Bettina, "I hope you think my offer is fair. Neither of us should keep the house. While I think I can afford it, I don't want to be there without you."

Mark started to outline his thoughts about support for Bettina. He knew that she would need help adjusting to being single again. Mark's lawyer had not said much; he seemed to be taking his cue from his client. Bettina was crumpled in the chair next to me, her chin tucked down and her eyes on the blank yellow legal pad in front of her. I hoped she could hear the kindliness in Mark's voice and his desire to still protect her, but I suspected she was too filled with discomfort, mortification, and fear to notice anything positive. Mark offered Bettina 30 percent of his gross salary for a period of 6 years and 60 percent of the proceeds from the sale of the home, together with half of the pension benefits accumulated during but not prior to the marriage.

This proposal was outside the box and more than reasonable in light of each party's resources. After a few other matters such as health and life insurance, a schedule for readying the house for sale, and selecting a real-estate broker, the meeting came to a civilized close. I told Mark's attorney that we would consider his offer and discuss who would draft the separation agreement, the document that would memorialize the amended marital obligations of the parties. Bettina straightened and moved toward the door without having contributed a word to the four-way meeting.

Fear can also be a deterrent to asking for a fair settlement. An abused woman with small children may say to her attorney, "Get me out of this marriage. I don't care what he pays me so long as it is something for the kids. He can have his electronic stuff, the truck, the stuff in the house, even the house. I'm afraid of him, his fists, and his anger. No matter what, I don't want to fight." Such a client does not care what she might be entitled to upon divorce. She can hardly stay in a lawyer's office long enough to find out what she is leaving on the negotiating table. She has calibrated the cost of possessions and support from this man and has chosen an outcome, despite its patently skimpy contours.

Timing is critical in the management of any case, especially when guilt, fear, and anger are present. Anger is often just below the surface of guilt, and if allowed to emerge, the guilty party can lose patience, begin to rationalize his or her conduct, and start feeling a lot less sympathetic and generous. Whenever I represent a wounded woman like Bettina, I urge a rapid settlement: The first offer is almost always the best one. She should catch the settlement at the crest of Mark's guilt, which almost always comes early in the case and wanes if months go by. I also tried to counsel Mary Ann to settle rapidly, as did her therapist and a lawyer to whom I sent her for a second opinion to emphasize the generosity of Vin's offer. But she insisted that she had to speak out, even though she would have endured less pain had she not gone to trial. I urged my hurting client to ignore her psychic pain and look at the situation in practical terms. She will have a lifetime to come to terms with her pain if she can sidestep it temporarily. Often the hurt will lessen after the stress of anticipating "the worst," when the final divorce judgment has been entered and the pain can diminish and healing and hope can surface.

On the other hand, moving a case slowly may be essential to ensure a reasonable settlement. People may need time to get past the guilt, anger, and fear that can cause overreaction. If Jane could be persuaded not to gallop headlong away from her abusive husband, Joe, maybe she would view her own conduct more charitably and her spouse's with less intense fear. Mothers with boyfriends all too often move out of the home before consulting with an attorney and then find that they should not have acted so hastily in light of their children's interests.

Managing clients' feelings requires different strategies depending on whether I am representing the guilt-ridden party or the wounded party. Whenever I represent the guilt-ridden party, I emphasize that divorce is no one's first choice, that love is not a feeling that can be compelled but only appreciated when present. There is often discontent on both sides, but one person becomes the self-appointed spokesperson for both parties' unhappiness. Guilt money doesn't lessen emotional hurt and pain; each party is entitled to compensation for past contributions to the marriage, and neither should walk away unduly impoverished. She or he may have become entangled with "a special friend" because of a real or perceived rejection by the spouse.

In my experience, the most critical determinant of any marriage's success or failure is the baggage the parties bring to the table. I always ask for a family history during the initial client conference; it is amazing how often the real ghosts are not the mates but the client's parents or the marriage model the client carries inside. Our understanding (or lack thereof) of "marriage" and "love" is set for us by our parents, and often one person's model is very different from his or her spouse's. I find that the family of origin as much as the client's own character and personality is the primary determinant of compatibility. I suspect that the spouse we pick to dance with is less important than the music we are dancing to internally.

I discuss this with receptive clients in the hope that seeing their behavior in a wider context will lessen their anger, disappointment, hurt, or guilt. I do not pretend to be a therapist, but I certainly tread in those waters when seeking to lessen guilt, hurt, and rage as the controlling forces. I try to help clients recognize that both parties have failed in the marriage dance. It is not one person's burden alone.

Finding the Box of Reasonable Settlement

Parties can locate the box of reasonable settlement by several paths:

- ❖ A couple may reach agreement on the box of reasonable settlement by themselves, without the assistance of any outsider.

❖ A couple may retain two attorneys to assist them in reaching a settlement.

❖ A couple may use a mediator to arrive at a resolution.

❖ A couple may use a mediator and separate attorneys as "coaches" to reach a reasonable settlement.

❖ A couple may appear in court with or without attorneys and be told by the judge what the box of reasonable settlement is in their case.

❖ A couple may use any combination of these methods.

Ninety-five percent of all divorce cases settle without the judge composing the terms of the settlement but only approving the settlement in the form presented. However, this figure does not reflect that some couples seek judicial assistance on one or more issues. Settlement occurs only when both sides agree upon the terms and conditions of the deal and agree to a new post-marital contract covering what will happen in aftermarriage. It is presented to the court for judicial approval and, if accepted, the marriage contract in its old form will terminate and an uncontested divorce judgment incorporating the revised agreement will be entered. If the couple is unable to reach agreement, the court will supply the new terms in the form of a judgment.

How to choose a process and proceed toward recasting the original marriage contract is the subject of the next several chapters. If the quality of aftermarriage is important, a divorcing person ought to make only reasonable offers of settlement. The most successful aftermarriage comes after both parties, carefully considering their specific circumstances, proceed in good faith and with an informed understanding of predictable, reasonable outcomes.

CHAPTER 8

Choosing a Process

Choosing the "right" divorce process is a challenge. Each option has advantages and disadvantages. The path of mediation may be the best process for some couples but not appropriate for others. Another couple may need the assistance of attorneys to level the playing field by correcting power imbalances in their relationship or unequal financial sophistication. Other couples will select the court process in light of their dynamics, the complexity of the issues, or their emotional agendas. In some cases, lack of financial resources may restrict choice, even to the point of precluding any professional advice.

The type of marital bargain does not necessarily determine the ideal path toward aftermarriage. It does, however, provide insight into the balance of power in the relationship. Perhaps the most significant factor in the choice of process is the quality of the communication between the divorcing parties at the time separation is sought. Where there is a comfortable level of communication, mediation may be the right choice; it is the least invasive approach with the maximum palliative possibilities. Where there is an extreme lack of communication and skepticism about the good faith of one or both of the parties, lancing the boil by litigation may be the only reasonable approach. Where divorcing couples are of unequal financial acumen or a power imbalance exists, retaining counsel can serve to balance the dynamics of the spousal relationship and may resolve financial misunderstandings, confusion, or lack of financial disclosure.

The Mediation Process

Zack's wife, Ginny, had decided that in the context of her complex marriage bargain, mediation was the appropriate divorce process. Although she was not sure what mediation entailed, it sounded conciliatory rather than adversarial. Ginny knew that she did not want to fight with Zack. They had both tried so hard to rekindle their passions. They had tried going on vacations to restore romance; they had been in couples' counseling for over a year. The spark, if ever present, eluded Ginny. Zack would have preferred to maintain the marriage facade. "Marriages do not demand sparkle," he had said to Ginny in their last counseling session.

In my second session with Ginny, I tried to educate her about the benefits and pitfalls of the mediation process. Beyond wanting to know the names of "good" mediators, Ginny wanted to know how the process worked and how to use it to her best advantage. She wondered who could serve as a mediator and what was the mediator's role.

Although mediators are usually persons with either a legal background or a social work background, or both, there are no uniform standards, or licensure procedures, to become a mediator. In many parts of the United States, anybody can declare himself, or herself, a mediator, with or without higher education or a background in the divorce process. The lack of uniform qualifications is a major problem with the process. While there are certification courses and a multitude of training programs available, the quality of mediators varies enormously.

I was relieved that Ginny wanted my assistance in selecting a mediator. I explained that the competence of the mediator is critical to the quality of the process. The role of the mediator is the subject of major disputes within the field of family law. Should the mediator's role be to assist the parties in reaching an agreement without reference to its fairness or the box of reasonable settlement? A mediation is all too often deemed successful when, and if, the parties reach the magical state of agreement, regardless of the quality of the final resolution. Who, if not the mediator, will monitor its reasonableness? The only safeguard in the process is the judge, who presides in a busy Family Court. A Family Court judge must approve the mediated agreement. The judge's review is often limited to a few minutes in a crowded courtroom where there are many other litigants waiting to be heard. Many judges are inclined to rubber stamp whatever deal the divorcing couple wants. All that the judge has to refer to is the written agreement; the two people; their affidavits that the marriage is over; and the parties' respective financial statements, which present only what the parties have willingly and voluntarily disclosed about their income, assets, and liabilities, even if signed under the pains and penalties of perjury.

I emphasized to Ginny how little supervision the mediation process afforded. Since mediation is a wholly voluntary process, it relies on the parties' willingness to produce complete financial information. There are no mechanisms to ensure that full financial disclosure has been made, such as are available through the court process. The mediation process presumes that the parties know how to "do the right thing" and that they want to do so. If valuations and appraisals are needed, the couple must know where and how to hire necessary experts. Parties too often assume that their mediator is overseeing the process and will tell them what to do and when to take an action. Unfortunately, there are mediators who do not require parties to obtain essential valuations of marital assets. In certain instances, the blame may rest with the unwillingness of the couple to incur the expense, the potential problems of knowing too little or too much, and not with the mediator. In other instances, the failure to inquire rests with the mediator's incompetence or even ignorance of the true nature of the marital assets.

The process is impaired when full and complete financial information has not been presented, for whatever reason. Where each of the spouses is a wage-earner, not self-employed or a participant in a complicated business where compensation varies enormously and can be "fudged" or "fixed," voluntary production of information works well together with a desire to be honest and forthcoming. The ideal couple should possess approximately the same level of financial sophistication and have parity of power in their relationship. If either person is effectively overbearing, then the other is disadvantaged. The dynamics of the marriage will not be altered in the mediation process.

When I had finished explaining the benefits and drawbacks of this process, Ginny wondered whether I was trying to discourage her from using mediation. I assured her that I was not opposed to using the mediation process for some kinds of cases. I admire couples who use the mediation process and believe that it is the least traumatic one when the circumstances are appropriate. This is the process that paves the way for the most constructive aftermarriage.

People contemplating divorce are letting go of their marriage in its familiar form. The mediation process is the least disruptive route if continuous dialogue is the yardstick. Couples who mediate must talk with each other in the mediation sessions. There may be strong disagreements and intense exchanges, but the process demands that they talk to one another face to face. This contrasts with what happens with alarming frequency when people go to court seeking resolution. The adversarial dynamic of a plaintiff and defendant, represented by attorneys (or not), takes over. The couple talks to each other only through counsel, rather than directly. This route may be necessary where communication has already failed or where it would be destructive to continue in mediation. However, where there is a chance of constructive communication, mediation encourages growth.

Couples who choose mediation must understand what it is that they are mediating: the financial dissolution of their marriage partnership and their future relationships with children and other family members, not their relationship. Unfortunately, people in mediation confuse agendas. An extreme, but not unusual, example is when one spouse still believes that the intact marriage can be saved were he, or she, to utter the perfect words.

All too often the parties are not only negotiating for or against a different goal, but also about a different subject matter. Women, in particular, tend consciously, or unconsciously, to negotiate their marital relationship rather than their financial best interests whereas their partner is seeking the best financial package. If men are concerned with a relationship being "at stake," it is more likely their relationship with their children, not the wife. A man often fears, and sometimes with very good reason, that his wife will restrict access, or worse, withhold the children in retaliation for his rejection of the marriage relationship. Mediation is a place where not only legal issues are at stake but also the complexities of the multitude of family ties and relationships. The possibility that one or both parties may be confusing their agendas is ever present.

I am worried about Ginny using the mediation process for just this reason. She feels the red hot button of guilt. She is the one calling an end to their marriage. She is asking Zack for a divorce that he does not want. Their grown children are certainly saddened by her wishes. Ginny wants to cause as little further damage to the family as is humanly possible. She is prepared to move out of the family home, since she reasons she is the one wanting to get out of the marital relationship. Ginny agreed with Zack when he had said, "You want to stop being married and I don't. Go, if you want. I'm not stopping you, just do not try to push me around."

Ginny tells me Zack's attitude works for her. She will use part of her inheritance to buy a house in the city. Ginny explains herself as follows, "I am bored in the suburbs. I grew up in the city, and I miss city life. I'm sick of driving 20 minutes to anywhere, even a supermarket. Zack can keep everything, including the lawn and the gardening. I've had enough mulching for a lifetime!"

Even though on the surface it seems that Ginny and Zack headed toward the same goal, they are not always mediating the same subject and do not have the same value system at work. Zack is eager to obtain the best financial package. Ginny is operating with many agendas simultaneously. In her mind, she is juggling her own guilt, Zack's anger, their children's disappointment, and, somewhere among these forces, her financial settlement. Her goal is to obtain as much permission from Zack to leave the marriage as money will buy. Her reward, she hopes, will be fewer complaints in the future from either Zack or the children about the terrible thing she has done to the family. Ginny calculates, quite openly with me, that if she leaves her husband the house, its contents, all his earned income, all his business interests, and his pension on the table for him to take, then he would be less outraged at her departure. Their grown kids will not think she was "grabby," a term she abhors, nor that she took "Dad to the cleaners." "Nickel and dime-ing Zack is not my *modus operandi*," she declared, with a wry smile and twinkling eyes.

On the surface, this suggested that Ginny desired to avoid a contentious aftermarriage. In the long run, however, I knew this to be a recipe for disaster in aftermarriage. A successful aftermarriage, like a successful marriage, must be built on a rational and equitable foundation.

How could I persuade Ginny that she was overreacting to her own emotions rather than rationally assessing the functions of the mediation process? The mediation process relies on each member in the couple asking for what he, or she, believes is fair in terms of finances, not emotional content. Her proposal for settlement was outside the box of reasonable settlement and would be one that Zack will eagerly agree to, resulting in a mediated agreement. Ginny had her own box of reasonable settlement, but it was bottomed on sentiment.

My task was made more difficult by Ginny's lack of understanding of Zack's complicated business interests, combined with her complete lack of desire to learn about the finances at this juncture in their relationship. Her attitude was that his business life had never interested her even when she was fully committed to him, so how could she pretend to care now? Probing into the financial details of the marriage also offended her sense of morality and fair play. She was satisfied with living off her inheritance; she believed it was sufficient for her needs. She also feared that asking Zack intrusive questions (by her, her lawyer, or anyone else) was a sure-fire recipe for cooking up his anger. I was not to do that! Her way made much more emotional sense to her and, in her view, had integrity, a trait she valued highly.

My concern for Ginny's financial fate in a mediation process intensified as the minutes ticked on. Given her utter lack of interest in Zack's financial dealings, my goal of moving her toward the box of reasonable settlement was not likely to be reached. Surely any mediator would be similarly handicapped by a wife who foreclosed inquiry and a husband who preferred silence or minimum disclosure. Even a proactive mediator, willing to deviate from strict neutrality, would be compromised by this couple's dynamics.

Ginny wanted my services as her mediation coach but wanted no action on my part. However, my job as her coach was to ensure that she was mediating with full financial information, that appraisals had been obtained where necessary, that assets had been appraised at full fair market value, that she was asking for what she wanted, and that her request was within the box of reasonable settlement. As I was precluded by her from doing my coaching job, and she was adamant about not taking my advice, we amicably parted company shortly after our third meeting.

While a mediated agreement can ease the passage from marriage to aftermarriage, it does not guarantee a financially reasonable and fair resolution. It may work at cross-purposes to achieving such a result as is demonstrated by Ginny and Zack. The cooperative nature of the process can allow a party driven by guilt or regret to agree to a settlement that ultimately they will resent.

Despite its pitfalls, I am a great advocate of mediation for suitable divorcing couples. Mediation is perfectly designed for well-informed, honest, employed spouses who can communicate with each other.

Knowing what you want and having realistic expectations in mediation (and probably in life generally) is power. If you do not know what you want, you cannot mediate effectively. Ginny and Zack appeared to know what they each wanted, but Zack was driven by resentment and Ginny by guilt. While they might be able to reach a mediated agreement at this time, experience has taught me that the harmony would be short-lived. By contrast, the companion couple, Natalie and Martin, each knew what they wanted: time with their children. Each understood the need for rationally based compromise. Were they to mediate their child-sharing arrangements, they would each have the same subject matter in mind and be very clear of their goal: time with the children. They might not agree on how to child share, at least initially, or even after several sessions, but they would be equally equipped to discuss the same problem. Moreover, they would have realistic expectations about the hard work necessary to reach their goal.

Divorcing couples who successfully mediate their unraveling marriages feel empowered by the process. They experience the ability to resolve smoothly the transition from marriage to aftermarriage as a vindication of their own decency and dignity. Very few couples who mediate their divorce find themselves unable to begin the task of working together in their rearranged marriage. They are buoyed by the experience of negotiating the financial aspects of disentanglement. They finish the mediation process with sufficient emotional reserves to address the realignment of their relationship in aftermarriage.

Collaborative Law Process/Negotiation Process

In the collaborative law model, the couple and their attorneys agree at the outset not to use the court process. They commit to negotiating a settlement agreement. If issues emerge that are irresolvable, they will designate another lawyer (a neutral person acting as a judge) to decide the dispute. The label "collaborative law process" is fairly new, but the process has long been in use. Many divorces are settled by two able lawyers who negotiate the outcome with each other, often with the assistance and in the presence of their clients. The statistic that 95 percent of all cases settle without trial reflects the prevalence of negotiated settlement agreements.

Ginny and Zack might have been better served by using the collaborative law process to resolve their financial issues. It is a process that avoids litigation without the risks of mediation. Had Ginny used the collaborative law process, her attorney would have insisted on full disclosure of financial information and on obtaining valuations where necessary. Ginny might still have chosen to agree to take less than her lawyer advised, but she would have done so with full knowledge of Zack's financial situation.

Negotiation between able attorneys and their clients can dismantle not only informational imbalances but also a power imbalance in a couple. In protectorate marriage bargains, such as Bettina and Mark's, the need to alter the power dynamic of the marriage is often critical. Had Bettina entered a mediation process, she would have been unable to be her own best advocate, given her self-image and the pattern of her relationship with Mark. As Mark was employed by a hospital, valuation of his medical practice was not an issue. Had Mark been a self-employed physician, or a physician working in a group medical practice, the financial issues would have been more complex and another reason to favor a negotiated settlement with the assistance of lawyers and access to a verification process.

The Court Process

The court process is invoked by divorcing people as a last resort. It is seldom the path of first choice for reasons that will be more fully detailed in later chapters. Divorcing couples find themselves in litigation when cooperation and good faith have disappeared. Although only 5 percent of all divorce cases result in a full trial of the parties' divorce, many more cases weave in and out of courts during their journey to aftermarriage.

The judicial process is the necessary choice where the divorcing couple is at an impasse. The impasse can occur while parties reside under the same roof or after the couple have physically separated. Vin (and his attorney) knew that Mary Ann was not going to cooperate in the demise of her classic marriage bargain. She would never agree to mediation or to retaining a lawyer unless and until Vin took definitive action that virtually forced her to see a lawyer. Likewise, an abused spouse may have no sensible alternative to the court process as direct or even indirect contact with his or her abuser is fraught with danger and fear.

Reasons to use the court process may emerge after the divorce process has begun. A person may refuse to pay support at a reasonable level or in a timely fashion. A person may refuse to fully disclose income or assets. Requests for financial information may be ignored or answered incompletely. The authority of the court may be the only way to correct the problem. The threat of "going to court" often empowers attorneys to make effective demands and is often the spur for successful negotiations. Attorneys bargain, negotiate, and make demands for financial information or cooperation in the shadow of the court process. Many cases settle on the eve of trial, at numbers not so very different from earlier numbers because it is hard to let go until one's back is to the wall. A court date serves as a wall against further procrastination and delay.

In considering which process to select in the journey from marriage to aftermarriage, each spouse must candidly evaluate the following factors:

* Quality of the marital relationship at the time of separation
* Extent of good faith
* Extent of trust
* Ability to communicate

- ❖ Power balance in relationship
- ❖ Financial knowledge and understanding, together and relative to each other
- ❖ Nature of the marital assets and liabilities
- ❖ Complexity of valuation of marital assets and liabilities
- ❖ Cost of process
- ❖ Impact of process on aftermarriage in the short term
- ❖ Impact of process on aftermarriage in the long term

A divorcing couple's aftermarriage experience may be far kinder and gentler if the choice of process is unswervingly tailored to curing problems rather than creating additional ones. We will revisit the impact of choice of process on aftermarriage in the short and long term in later chapters. A mediated agreement or a negotiated settlement agreement (also called a separation agreement) can address a far wider range of issues and in much greater depth than any court order or judgment (see Chapter 12, "Making a Deal"). The court process can only lead to either an "order" or a "judgment" (for information on orders, see Chapter 10, "The First Skirmish," and on judgment, see Chapter 13, "A Judgment Is Only a Judgment").

CHAPTER 9

Child Sharing

While divorcing parents remain "parents forever," they may not remain actively present in their children's lives after divorce. How a couple manages its physical disentanglement can impact forever the quality of the children's relationship with one parent or both. The idea that divorce is a part of marriage, rather than an end to marriage, may help parents take a longer view in designing their child-sharing arrangements.

The fact of divorce does not alter one iota the existence of the parent/child relationship. Each of the parents is just as much a parent as she, or he, was before that dreadful day. All that the granting of a divorce has achieved is to effect a change in the physical proximity and access of parents to their children. After parents physically separate, neither parent will necessarily have physical proximity or access to the children one hundred percent of the time.

All too often the divorce process is seen as the perfect opportunity for one parent, or both, to rewrite the parenting story. Sometimes a father wants to become even more involved with the children than before the separation. A mother may claim that a father has been a negative, even destructive, influence and she needs to protect her children from his damaging influence. She wants to use the separation and ensuing divorce as her opportunity to monitor the quality of his fathering and curtail its amount. These impulses, while understandable, may only serve to confuse and upset the children. They are counterproductive to any hope for a smooth journey to aftermarriage.

A Statute Without Custody

In the recently revised, and enacted, "Family Law Act 1996" in Britain, the word "custody" and its connotations of possession have been eliminated. Instead, the statute sets forth the principle that both parents have the same rights with respect to the children as when the marriage was intact. The destructive and divisive consequences to parents and children of determining "legal," "physical," "sole," and "joint custody" are avoided. Instead, the parents dispute territory and access to the children. The British family courts have authority to enter "residence orders," "access orders," and "maintenance orders" for the support of the spouse and children, but no order granting an award of children to a parent. Access to children may be problematic after physical separation of the parents. However, that difficulty is not exacerbated by the charged labels of custodial and visiting parent.

Thousands of litigation dollars will be saved by separated and divorced parents who can concentrate on fighting territorial battles for possession of a residence rather than the custodial battles for "possession" of the children, using the inflammatory labels of sole legal custody versus joint legal custody and/or sole physical custody versus joint physical custody.

The British approach to parenting in aftermarriage is refreshingly original and in sharp contrast to its historical antecedents in the Common Law. In early English law a father owned his children, just as he owned all property of the marriage. Upon divorce, he had sole legal and physical custody of the children, as well as all other property. Under more recent law in England and in the United States, the court had the power to reassign the care, companionship, and custody of the children to the mother or father upon divorce. In all state statutes of divorce in the United States, there are provisions for "custody" and its award to one parent or the other or both parents, jointly. In some jurisdictions, there is a presumption of joint legal custody unless facts warrant a finding of sole custody.

The former British paradigm, and all American counterparts of the Act, set the power struggle around the issue of custody. The revised and recently amended British Act sets the power struggle around victory or loss of the residential order. The party who "wins" the marital residence wins the children because continuity of residence is nearly always paramount. The same fight is being waged but with different legal nomenclature. I prefer to have the parties argue only about a dwelling rather than possession, control, and ownership of children. It feels healthier. It also provides hope that the parent/child relationship will not be fractured because of divorce.

Divorce statutes in the United States set the power struggle around custody of the children. Although there may be plenty of fighting over the marital residence, that becomes secondary to winning "possession" or at least "primary possession" of the children. Parents would be wise to reframe their thinking about how to share the children along the lines of the British paradigm that emphasizes the continuity of the parent/child relationship. The following description of my representation of Natalie, the wife of Martin in a companion marriage bargain, illustrates some of the difficulties of designing child-sharing arrangements and then living with those plans. The problems are only compounded by empty arguments over labels.

Shared Parenting: Natalie and Martin

My third meeting with Natalie required considerable care and instruction. It occurred just before a scheduled four-way meeting with Martin and his attorney. The purpose of the four-way meeting was to discuss living arrangements in light of the parties' impending physical separation.

Natalie and Martin, a companion couple, were still living under the same roof with their children, Michael, aged 10, and Nicole, aged 8. Natalie hoped that I would make Martin move out; the tension at home was intense. Just yesterday, Michael's teacher had remarked to Natalie that Michael seemed to be having trouble concentrating on schoolwork. Natalie had noticed how often Nicole talked to her with a whine and then followed by sucking her thumb, a habit the child had long ago discarded.

Natalie looked exhausted. Her makeup did not hide the dark circles under her green eyes. I could feel her inner turmoil and distress as she sighed and began our meeting with the following, "What are you going to say to Martin and his attorney about moving out and about custody? The children need to know what will happen to them. They know that we are divorcing, and they are really confused."

Preparing Natalie for the difficulties of child sharing in aftermarriage was a daunting task; her expectations about what a divorce would do for her were romantic and unrealistic. I started by explaining that custody battles are really battles about power and control between the separating parties, not about children. Children are always best served by the absence of any argument about their care. Each parent should honor and respect the importance of the other parent for the sake of the children. Friction, tension, and anger around sharing children only produce harm to all concerned, and it is far less important where a child puts his head on the extra or odd night (usually Wednesday or Sunday) than that there be no fighting about the issue.

Natalie stopped me and asked, "Is going back and forth between homes healthy for children? I believe that they need a primary residence."

All too often I have heard one parent, usually the mother, express her concern about a child having to go back and forth between two homes, even if it happens only once a week. She invariably characterizes the swap as a horrible disruption. Yet the genuine cause of problems in sharing children comes from the discomfort of one or both of the parents with the fact of sharing. Transitions are difficult for everyone, but that has nothing to do with the specific schedule and everything to do with the parents' decision to be separated. The particular pattern of child sharing is not nearly as important as the parents' attitude and goodwill toward each other expressed by their desire that their children be with both parents. Natalie needed to accept, fully, the inevitable consequences of a physically rearranged family. Child sharing would be a key concept in her aftermarriage just as it had been in her marriage.

Parenting in aftermarriage, like parenting in marriage, requires cooperation between parents. The degree of harmony and goodwill needs to be even greater in a fractured family than in an intact marriage as a counterweight to the inevitable obstacles of time and space. The court seeks to enter an order that mirrors the patterns of the family prior to the filing of the divorce action. The essential inquiry is, "How did the parents "parent" the children before they appeared in court or prior to the settlement negotiations? Who was home with the children? Who took the children to the doctor, dentist, and extracurricular activities? Were the child-related tasks shared or was one parent primarily responsible?" The court seeks to change as little as possible for the children upon divorce. Aftermarriage parenting arrangements seek to replicate marriage parenting arrangements as closely as possible. The ideal is a seamless transition from the marriage to aftermarriage. Of course, continuation of the past arrangement is a fantasy given the new dynamic of parents living apart. Yet as much as possible, activities that were done with each parent prior to the fracturing of the family should be maintained in an uninterrupted way.

I warned Natalie that a father's request for equal time with the children will be heard with sympathy and approval. Most judges welcome a father who wants to see and enjoy his children. They are more accustomed to fathers whose energies are spent avoiding parental obligations. Judges appreciate an involved father: an antidote to the many, many cases of nonsupport and absence. A mother's dissatisfaction with her spouse's parenting skills occurs quite often as a misguided reaction to her own pain and suffering at having been left. Her real agenda may be to use the child-sharing arrangements as a means of spousal punishment, a form of retaliation. And that is a recipe for disaster in the transition from marriage to aftermarriage.

Natalie seems to be still listening, even though I am delivering a bitter pill. Her self-control and polite demeanor disguise her apprehension and disappointment. Have my words changed her attitude, I wonder? Natalie is right in saying that the family might be better served if one of the parents moves out. Delay has only caused the household level of anger to increase.

Natalie and Martin have relatively young children, and they will need to be (or become) flexible and forgiving about changes to whatever child-sharing arrangement they adopt at the start. Children change and grow as do their needs, interests, and concerns. A rigid adherence to a set schedule is not realistic. Special events, trips, and activities invariably disrupt the best laid plans. Parents who are divorced need to recognize that flexibility is extremely important. Compensatory time for missed visits will soften disappointments. Indeed, in the busy lives of companion couples, who often both have full time employment, the need for flexibility and adaptability is paramount. These qualities cannot be imposed by words on a piece of paper but must emerge from parents' realistic understanding of the struggles of child rearing, whether those struggles exist in an intact family or in a re-arranged family. The static, set quality of any child-sharing schedule conflicts with the need for fluidity and flexibility. While the parents (and children) may need and crave predictability, the system adopted must have some fluidity. As children change, their parents must be prepared to respond appropriately, and per-haps differently, depending upon the age and stage of the chil-dren involved.

There are very few caring divorced parents with two homes who feel that they see too much of their children. Were the par-ents under one roof, the constant splitting and sharing of time would evaporate as an issue. This "cost" of physical separation is unavoidable and must be measured as an "expense" of the jour-ney to aftermarriage. While the goal is constancy and replication of previous parenting patterns, that is also a fantasy. The arrange-ments can be carefully crafted, in fact perfectly measured and rea-sonable in light of the realities, but they are never as good as when the family was intact.

I showed Natalie a calendar with each day divided into four sections: morning, afternoon, evening, and night-time. I sug-gested that she think about how the children might be shared in any given week. What times in the past several months had the children been exclusively with her or exclusively with Martin? I asked her to think about her work, and nonwork, schedule. Did she regularly take a class on a particular evening or always go to an event each week? When was that time? If there were nights she was usually busy or alternatively that Martin was committed, those nights might be easy to assign. I suggested that each parent might want to have an entire weekend with the children so that a trip might be possible.

Soon after Natalie completed the calendar, both on a weekly basis and with monthly cycles, Martin and his attorney arrived at my offices. The four way meeting had been scheduled in an attempt to help the parents resolve how to separate and how to share the children after separation. Martin's attorney, Jeffrey Thomas, is an able, reasonable, and experienced lawyer who believed, as I did, that it was our task to help this couple avoid the court process if at all possible. We knew our clients were wonderful parents facing a complicated and painful situation with no easy and comfortable solution. We hoped that negotiation might rescue them from a head on collision in court. Prior to the conference, Mr. Thomas and I had discussed how we might broker an agreement. We would have our clients prepare proposed schedules without reference to the inflammatory "c" word. If we failed to arrive at an agreed schedule, we would then agree on a method for resolving our clients' differences. No judge could possibly gather as much information about this family from a brief court appearance as we had already learned. We had also discussed therapists who, in our past experiences, had been competent, responsive, and swift in meeting with clients and who were willing to serve as Guardians Ad Litem ("GAL") in a court proceeding. A Guardian Ad Litem is a person appointed by the court to assist the judge in determining the children's best interests. (The GAL prepares a written report that makes recommendations as to the most suitable child-sharing arrangements given the past history and present relationships of the various family members.)

Our aim was to persuade our clients to reach an acceptable child-sharing arrangement without the assistance of outside help beyond the two of us. As a fall back position, we would propose a short list of candidates to serve as a GAL. Using any expert would mean loss of control of how the rearranged family would live. We would stress to Natalie and Martin the benefits of retaining power over family decisions. If that failed, we would introduce the idea of adding a GAL to the negotiations. While having the power to pick who would make family decisions was not as desirable as working it out themselves, it was preferable to having a stranger, whom one did not select, make those intimate and significant decisions. Our clients could interview the short-listed candidates in leisure, ensure good chemistry, and find some peace of mind regarding his or her role in their lives.

As I explained to Natalie the agenda of our four-way meeting, I again emphasized the benefits of parental cooperation. The more that she and Martin could work together, the less they would find their private family matters interfered with by the State. She might have to give up a night or two, but she and her husband would be co-captains of their children's ship. If she insisted that there be only one captain, that person would be neither parent.

The four-way meeting began with Martin's attorney educating our clients about the number of cases that resolve without trial and how much we hoped that Natalie and Martin would be among the group of divorcing parents who handled their parenting issues amicably. After all, there were only two major sticking points: who would stay in the residence and how the children would be shared. The financial picture would fall into perspective when these two major issues were resolved.

Not long into the meeting, Natalie piped up with the rather testy remark that she had made all mortgage payments since Martin had become self-employed. Her superior financial circumstances meant she should stay in the house. I wished that she had remained silent as Martin then felt embarrassed and defensive. He pointed out that he had paid all the closing costs at the time of purchase and he was the parent who lived in the house, not on the road. Natalie's remark was provocative, irrelevant, and unlikely to facilitate reasonable further discussion.

In an attempt to get the meeting back on track, Martin's attorney proposed that we take our clients aside and return with concrete proposals for child sharing and separate living arrangements. Fifteen minutes later, the conference resumed. Martin proposed that they continue to reside under the same roof until after the holidays (two months away). Thereafter, he proposed that they divide the children's time equally between them. He suggested that the children spend one week with Natalie and the next with him; the change-over day could be Saturday or Sunday. Natalie and I had discussed sharing the week, with Martin having the children from Sunday morning until Tuesday morning since he took the kids to soccer on Sunday and coached his son's team. Saturday was the only day Natalie could really enjoy the children since the other days she worked and did not want to tread on Martin's Sunday schedule with the children.

Natalie thought her proposal was eminently reasonable, just as Martin thought his was. Natalie looked at Martin with venom: Martin avoided all eye contact with either his wife or me, preferring to stare out the window. Glaring at Martin, Natalie said, "I hate the thought of the children being a weekly 'ping pong' game. How would you like to change residences every week? Get real! The kids need to have one primary home and regular visits with you." Martin, without changing the focus of his eyes, said with steely precision, "The kids like being with me and you know it. Why should I have only the shank of the week?"

I tried to resurrect some harmony by saying, "At least you both agree that the time with the children should be shared and that is an important beginning. The next question is then, do you both want to keep the power to decide the details of the sharing? Would you be more comfortable with a therapist of your choosing making the recommendation as that is what will happen if the two of you cannot agree?"

I knew that Attorney Thomas had agreed with my comment since he began drawing up a monthly calendar, which he passed to his client. I drew a similar one and gave it to Natalie. We would try to harmonize the two schedules, if humanly possible.

After a few minutes, the clients gave each of their lawyers their child-sharing proposals in calendar form. Natalie's proposal had not changed and neither had Martin's. We, or rather our clients, were at loggerheads, and, therefore, Attorney Thomas and I moved on to the next agenda item: the choice of therapist to serve as GAL. After a further few minutes of talk, the three names proposed were agreed to by the parties; they agreed to interview the suggested therapists and let us know whom they liked the best.

The conflict-ridden issue of "territory" was the remaining agenda item. Martin made his position clear with the simple statement, "I am not moving. If Natalie wants to end the marriage, she can move. Besides she has more cash available than I have, so she can afford to go." Natalie responded with, "You are right. You have been getting a free ride at home, and now I want to stop supporting you. The kids and I will stay in the house, and you can find a place that you can afford. Why don't you find an apartment closer to the soccer field where you have to be every Sunday and where there are free outdoor tennis courts. You always hang out there anyway during the day."

The four-way meeting was nearing a logical ending, and Martin's attorney and I knew that we had only satisfactorily resolved one issue: a process for selecting a GAL. We had not resolved—or even come close to resolving—who would leave the home, if anyone. In the interim between receiving the report of the GAL and either parent departing the residence voluntarily, we proposed that our respective clients rotate on a regular evening basis who would be home with the children and who would have the night off. We suggested that Natalie and Martin minimize contact with the other in the hope that opportunities to argue could be reduced and tension lessened. Based on the activities of the family, we plotted out a proposed weekly schedule for the family while they all continued to live under one roof. As Natalie and Martin's children were due back from school within the hour, the four-way conference terminated.

The next day I spoke with Natalie. She was not pleased because nothing definitive had been decided as far as she was concerned, other than a writing commemorating the family's weekly pattern of activities and several people to interview. She was eager to move forward and relieve her frustration and distress. I was sympathetic, but I knew that her psychic pressure would not be lessened in the short-term unless she was the party to move out. I knew that moving out was unacceptable to her. Moving out also would negatively impact the ultimate financial outcome, as Martin could not pay her the value of her one-half interest in the home.

A week went by, and I again spoke with Natalie. I suggested that she and I meet to discuss strategy. She was at a cross-roads. She needed to think long and hard about which path was best for her, Martin, and the children—in the short and long term.

If she went the route of the GAL, she would lose control of the outcome. She would be stuck with a stranger's view of the children's best interests, albeit an expert stranger. If she chose mediation, she would remain involved in the decision-making process. However, she and I already knew from the four-way meeting that anything less than equal time with the children would be unacceptable to Martin. If Natalie agreed now to equal time with the children, the rest of the divorce arrangements might fall into place. A parenting coordinator, a person with a background in therapy, could be selected by the parties and given the permanent role of resolving future child-related differences. Such person would be named in the parties' settlement agreement, available not just during the divorce but also in the future, if and when child-related disputes arose. In contrast to a GAL, a parenting coordinator can stay with the couple over the years ahead, not just when the parties are before the court. I suggested to Natalie that if she could bring herself to agree to sharing the children equally with Martin, he might consider moving out of the house after the holidays. This plan would secure for Natalie the house as her territory. If we proposed a review of the child-sharing arrangements by the parenting coordinator in three months following his moving out, and again in six months or a year and yearly thereafter, there would be built in flexibility. Given reviews, the parents and children could then easily reconsider how the arrangement was working and in what ways the sharing arrangements could be improved. The reviews would happen after everybody had had a chance to experience life in a rearranged family.

If alternating weeks, as Martin had proposed, proved unwieldy or unworkable, she could suggest her preferred schedule of three nights with one parent, followed by four nights with the other. We both knew that less than perfect equality at this point in time would provoke a war from Martin. I buttressed my proposal with the comment that I thought the children would be relieved if they learned that matters had been settled between their parents and would welcome the "fairness" of the arrangement: equal time with each parent. Martin could never say to the children that Natalie had blocked his being with them, and more importantly, the children would never say to their mother that she had interfered with his time with them. Finally, I mentioned the enormous benefit of resolving their situation through an amicable negotiation that proceeded rapidly to resolution.

Natalie agreed to think about the three choices. She was disheartened to realize how much her companion marriage bargain colored her present situation. She acknowledged that the *classic* divorce pattern of a primary custodial parent and a visiting parent did not fit her circumstances. In parting, she said with a touch of humor, "How come I never realized that my high ideals of best friend marriage would, like a worm, turn into a forced friend divorce!"

The Guardian Ad Litem

English and American family court judges have the power and right to appoint an expert to assist them in determining the best interests of the children. Such expert (often a therapist or attorney with a social work background) is usually given the title and authority of a "Guardian Ad Litem." A Guardian Ad Litem's obligation is to file a written report for the judge. The report should describe the dynamics of the family, the conflicting interests, and his or her recommendations for resolution. The report is supposed to be confidential and protective of the privacy of the children and the parents—a "secret" of sorts. The wishes of the children are said not to control the final determination but are merely one of the many factors to be weighed by the Court. Children of parents in the process of divorce are usually, if not always, interviewed by the Guardian. Their statements, if any, are interpreted and then placed in the context of everything else the interviewer has come to learn about the family. The report often contains more information than just the fact of a meeting with the children; it speaks to the quality of the relationships among the family members; it often quotes remarks made by parents, children, and care-givers. The presiding judge, more often than not, just "rubber stamps" the recommendations without independent corroboration or affording counsel the opportunity to cross-examine. It is an imperfect system even at its best, but it is a means of side-stepping the horror of a full scale custody battle.

Neither Natalie nor Martin may be happy with the Guardian Ad Litem's solution to the family problem. The inability of Natalie and Martin to agree "on the children" has created a concrete, palpable source of bitterness to fan the flames of discord between the parents. Each parent may covet a piece of the schedule given to the other. The children know they are pawns, who have been evaluated by "a strange person" but ultimately not heard.

The Longer Perspective

As much, and as often, as I stress the realities of the alternatives to separating parents, I know that my beliefs and prejudices may not be heard. Even after I explain the disadvantages of losing so much control and power to a stranger who views the assignment as "work" and the advantages of working this out with a spouse who knows and loves the children, I may fail to persuade.

For the sake of the harmony of the aftermarriage, I hope that direct confrontation can be avoided. Children are hurt the most in divorce by friction, not where they spend their Wednesday or Sunday night. I will continue to try to persuade Natalie of this fact. Perhaps Natalie and Martin can be persuaded to try mediation on the issue of child sharing if they cannot now decide what to do. Mediation would give these two a chance to discuss how to work cooperatively from a distance, now and in the future. They could use mediation on parenting issues or better yet a parenting coordinator to help them verbalize to each other their aftermarriage expectations. Parenting in aftermarriage requires greater communication, more attention to details, greater teamwork, and more tolerance of unpleasant transitions and adjustments than in an intact marriage. Neither Martin nor Natalie expected that after their intact marriage ended, they would forever be in this hidden marriage, called aftermarriage.

Protecting Children

The laws of marriage and divorce recognize that children of parents who have split need greater protection than children of an intact marriage. Family law presumes that a child of an intact family requires the least protection; a child of unwed parents requires the most protection and children of divorce somewhere in the middle. These distinctions are based on the assumption that married parents will be able both to agree on child-related issues and to keep as a centerpiece of their deliberations the best interests of the family if not the children. Parents who are separated and divorced, it is assumed, cannot be counted on to consider the needs of their children in the same way as married couples. Children of separated or divorcing parents, therefore, are thought to need greater protection from the silent partner of the marriage, the State.

Children of an intact marriage cannot use the court process to champion their right to higher education and payment therefor, necessary and usual medical care such as orthodonture, or therapy. In contrast, children of divorce have the right to compel the payment of these expenses from a parent who can afford to pay. Children of divorced or divorcing parents who are of the age of majority may bring suit in their own name against a parent for nonsupport, medical expenses, and insurance.

Children of unwed parents have even greater rights against their parents than children of divorce and, of course, children of parents in an intact marriage. Again, the assumption is that the child's best interests will not be paramount in the parents' agenda. The State is yet more present in an out-of-wedlock child's life than in that of children of marriage or aftermarriage. A child of unwed parents may bring suit in his or her own name, even before attaining the age of majority in some jurisdictions. In the past quarter century, the relationship of parent and child has been radically realigned due to the perceived need for protection of a child who lacks married parents.

CHAPTER 10

The First Skirmish

Many people wonder how and when they will go to court. How soon does it happen and under what circumstances? How does a case go from selecting an attorney to going before a judge? How often does one have to go to court before the divorce is finished?

In most cases, a couple's first introduction to the judicial system occurs at the temporary order stage. Following the initial conference and any subsequent meetings, lawyer and client determine the most appropriate course of action for disentangling the parties. Some couples avoid temporary orders by reaching agreement through mediation or even negotiating a complete settlement, and appear in court only at the end of the process to obtain judicial approval of their agreement.

The most sensible approach is usually to work slowly, cautiously hoping to broker a peaceful settlement. Seldom are children and the "wounded" spouse as emotionally ready to move on as the spouse who wants the separation and divorce. With Mary Ann and Vin, Eleanor and Henry, Natalie and Martin, Bettina and Mark, and Ginny and Zack, the need for a slow start was evident. However, a slow start requires that spouses agree that all household expenses and ordinary and usual bills will be paid as before.

Time is taken to collect financial information and discuss the physical separation and the sharing of the children. Usually no court intervention seeks to accelerate this process, and this can take several months. Progress in most divorce cases is far more deliberate than most people expect, which is especially frustrating for the spouse for whom the marriage is definitely *over*.

An emergency hearing immediately following the initial client conference can occur when there are exceptional circumstances dictating a swift response: a parent removing the children from the home (or state, or country) without the other parent's consent, an episode of physical violence, likely to recur, necessitating immediate protective orders for the victim, or a refusal to pay support to the family.

Points of Conflict

These are the major points of conflict, or sticking points, at the beginning of the divorce process:

1. Who will stay in the house?
2. How will the children be cared for and by whom?
3. Can one spouse demand that the other vacate the house?
4. How will the children be supported?
5. Will there be any support for the spouse and, if so, how much?
6. Who is responsible for the debts of the marriage?
7. Can the assets of the marriage be preserved during the divorce?
8. Who should be responsible for attorneys' fees?

Purpose and Effect of Temporary Orders

The temporary order stage, which comes after filing the complaint for divorce and before the trial, is for many clients their first whiff of litigation. It is educational and often sobering, particularly if a client expects the court process to solve all of his or her problems. Sometimes I suggest that a client spend a morning watching other people present their domestic problems before a congested and impersonal Family Court, so their expectations will be closer to reality. Usually my client will see someone presenting the same issues as he has, as many litigants have the identical concerns at the outset of any case.

Temporary orders are intended to tide the parties over, addressing a multitude of financial, custodial, or residential problems that emerge during the dissolution. Some common ones include temporary restraining orders that freeze assets, temporary custody or visitation orders, temporary support orders of children and/or spouse, temporary orders to vacate marital residence, orders to produce documents, or orders to pay counsel fees or other specific bills.

Temporary orders create meaningful precedents in both settlement discussions and at trial, setting the stage for permanent orders of custody, support, and residence—absent a major change in circumstances or a gross misrepresentation of the earned or unearned income of one or both spouses.

Preparing for Court and the Courthouse

Before arriving at court, both sides prepare and exchange motions, such as a motion for temporary custody or support, a motion to vacate, a restraining order, or a motion for counsel fees, to name a popular few. The motions are often accompanied by affidavits or memoranda in support and the parties' mandatory financial statements, which the court needs when making child-related, monetary, and residential orders. What are the financial resources of the parties, and how much earned and unearned income does each of the parties have? How valuable are the parties' assets, and how much is in their individual and joint checking and savings accounts? What debts burden the parties?

How much money do the parties need to meet their reasonable living expenses? Is there any surplus in the budget? Constancy is what is sought for the children who are seen as innocent victims and the court's responsibility to protect.

Many court systems have mediators or family-services officers with whom litigants must meet prior to gaining a hearing before the presiding judge to conserve limited judicial resources, promote settlement, and ensure that the issue presented in court has been previewed by a knowledgeable person. Only the implacable cases move past the screening process, almost like in a doctor's office where a nurse performs routine tests and an initial diagnosis before an actual physician comes in.

Most people going through a divorce have never been in a courtroom, and more often than not, it is a rude awakening to the process's lack of dignity, privacy, and personal concern for the sentiments of the litigants. Courtrooms are often overcrowded and corridors filled with anxious humanity sprawled on benches or window ledges, impatient to be done with the unpleasant business at hand. The buildings are often plain, grimy, and in need of renovation, with an air of tension and anxiety.

The courthouse is a place I know well, however. I am accustomed to its appearance, commotion, and smell. I like the time in the hallway as we wait our turn on the various court lists. It is not exactly jovial, but it is social; I can settle another case, see a law-school acquaintance, remind a fellow attorney to confirm an agreement in writing, or gossip with colleagues. I enjoy being out of the office and having a chance to circulate. Presenting a temporary order in the motion session, compared to a day in the trial session, is not stressful for me. I have argued most motions on many occasions; the facts may be new but the issues are familiar, and the motion session ambience is informal compared to the formalities of a trial.

Mary Ann and Vin's Motion Session

Mary Ann and I were in the motion session as a result of my filing motions for temporary support and for counsel fees. Mary Ann had not received any support from Vin for the past two months, and his lawyer refused to address this issue with me. Vin's lawyer also avoided discussing payment of Mary Ann's legal fees, which she could ill afford given her paltry salary as an elementary school teacher. Vin had stopped paying the mortgage on their expensive condominium after Mary Ann rejected his offer of settlement. The last check Mary Ann had received was for $2,000, which she spent on "the boys"—their food and money to travel back to college—and the utility bills at the condominium.

"How does Vin expect me to pay for the condo? We bought it only last year after we sold our big house to help pay for college," Mary Ann said to me after we took our places on the hard benches in the hallway outside of the courtrooms. She was nervous as we waited to see the family-services officer. The family-services officer would try to mediate an agreement on all the issues raised in our motions, and only if unsuccessful, would the matter be heard by the presiding judge of the motion session. Of course, mediation was delayed until all parties and counsel were present. Mary Ann looked especially nice in a beige skirt and blue silk blouse, with a lovely necklace peeking out at the collar. I had suggested that she not wear anything too fancy, since she was trying to convince the court that she was in need of support. Mary Ann's left foot swung back and forth furiously as we sat. We were fifth on the list.

Vin and his lawyer had not been interested in a four-way meeting until we had exchanged financial information. Vin's lawyer, Attorney James, said Vin was working on his financial statement and he would get it to me when it was ready. I had called him three times and heard the same line, and each time I reminded him of my client's pressing financial circumstances and his client's failure to pay support. After the third time, I knew other action was necessary. In the fourth call, I said, "Vin has not paid anything other than what he gave her two months ago. She is out of money and the mortgage is past due. We cannot wait any longer, given the lack of a settlement agreement, or progress toward a settlement. I have no choice. I have marked up motions for hearing. You will be receiving two in the mail: one motion for support and one for counsel fees."

I had spoken with a court clerk, and three weeks later was the earliest I could get this case on the overcrowded docket list. This was my first case with Attorney James, and so far I was unimpressed with his punctuality—he was 20 minutes late, and I knew the delay would drop our case to the bottom of the list. I was increasingly disenchanted with his relaxed attitude, particularly in light of my client's justifiable financial anxiety. Mary Ann and I waited and watched the list of family-service cases swell. At last Mary Ann pointed to two men marching into family services to report their presence in the courthouse.

After a few minutes they emerged and stood next to the window at the far end of the hallway, still seemingly oblivious to our presence. Vin stepped away for a moment, and I left Mary Ann on the bench and approached Attorney James.

I introduced myself and said, "Maybe you could step into my 'office'"—a vacant spot just outside the room where the other clients and their lawyers were milling around. I asked Attorney James if he was prepared to exchange financial statements and whether he had a support figure in mind. Attorney James looked down at me from his full six feet, readjusted his pants (which looked a bit too tight on his former football-player build), and said in an easy manner, "Take a look at his financial statement.

He is not making any money with the copy business. I do not know how the guy is eating. He is living in a one-bedroom apartment that costs him over $1,000 a month—he has no extra cash. He is hurting."

"Take a look at *her* financial statement!" I said, as he bent down to hear me. "She's a schoolteacher and lives in Green Valley, where the common fees are over $300 a month and the mortgage is over $4,000 per month."

We swapped financial statements and agreed to spend a few minutes looking at the financial statements with our clients. Not surprisingly, Mary Ann was disgusted by Vin's statement. She said, "He's lying. He took a vacation with Jill to the Bahamas a month ago, he's driving a red sports car—he has money. Look at what he's wearing—that's a new suit! I can't even get the boys new sneakers. How can he do this to the boys?"

She commented on each and every entry on Vin's financial statement, from his income to the cost of his apartment to his entertainment expenses of $45 per week for himself and the boys.

"He has not seen the boys for a month. He told me he and his partner had set their draw at $1,000 a week. I can't believe he's now reporting $500 a week. Anita, what am I going to do? I can't live on the street! We can't sell the condo—the mortgage is $450,000, and the most we would get in this market is $330,000, if we were lucky."

She opened her purse and pulled out a Kleenex, blew her nose, readjusted her slight body and turned to me. "What are you going to do, Anita?"

Not a whole lot, I thought to myself. I would lay out the painful circumstances to the judge as vociferously as I could. It was a real mess, and I knew it would only get worse. Vin may have had twinges of guilt, but even a realistic, generous offer, even if he contributed his entire draw, would not cover the boys' expenses and the mortgage.

I took the financial statements back across the room to where Attorney James was standing with Vin. This was my first opportunity to meet Vin (he had gone to get a cup of coffee out of the vending machine), and I introduced myself. Vin was wearing a polyester blue striped suit, red and blue tie, and a pink buttoned down shirt. He was an attractive, short man with lovely blue eyes and an enormous dimple that came alive as he smiled and greeted me. He did not look a day over 40. He and Mary Ann made a "cute couple," I thought to myself, and looked as if they belonged together. I asked Attorney James to come back to our corner to talk.

When we were alone, I said, "I need Mary Ann to receive $400 a week and the mortgage and condo fees paid by Vin. She will not accept anything less, and I do not blame her. I know that the child support guidelines call for less, a lot less, but her expenses are over the top. The shortfall between the amount I am looking for and the guideline amount, we could label alimony." I added that Mary Ann was not a frivolous lady—she was a real saver—but there was no way she could manage, and she certainly could not pay my attorney fees. Whatever retainer he received from Vin, I would ask the judge to order as my counsel fees.

"I wish I could offer you that," he said, "but Vin just does not have that kind of dough. They have to sell the condo and the sooner they do the better. We both know the court will not order the real estate sold at the temporary order stage, but if they do not do it now, they'll only be further underwater."

He was right, I knew, but Mary Ann would not be compliant. She was in a precarious mental state even without the stress of a move, and she would not do it to the boys. When I returned to the bench, Mary Ann said, "Vin knew what he was doing when we bought the condo. I never should have agreed to sell the other house, which was almost fully paid off. I do not know what Vin did with all the proceeds—we only put down $50,000 on the condo."

Family services called our case. In some courthouses, the lawyers go in alone, then the clients come in after the lawyers have explained the facts to the family-services officer. In this courthouse, it was our choice, and Attorney James and I agreed to go in without Vin and Mary Ann. I knew this case was not going to be successfully mediated and the faster we got upstairs to see the judge, the less time we would waste. If we were lucky, we would be heard before the lunch break.

Joanne was a competent, experienced family-services officer who had been in the court system at least 10 years. We told her the score: Neither one of us thought this case could be mediated; the parties were just too far apart. Joanne said, "Oh, come on. Let me try. You never know."

Attorney James and I looked at each other, artificial smiles forming, and I began to tell Mary Ann's story. I told her this is a marriage of 23 years, with two children aged 19 and 21, both at Ivy League colleges on partial scholarships; the wife is a primary school teacher … and so on, followed by the financial realities, the parties' actual expenses and reported incomes according to today's financial statements. Attorney James was gracious enough to shorten the meeting by saying, "I agree with Anita's summary of the facts. I would only add that Vin has several business loans that I have listed on Schedule B of his financial statement, totaling $300,000. He and his partner are in the midst of expanding the business with the hope that the new location will generate additional income after the initial build-out investment."

Joanne understood that she was not going to resolve the case, but felt that she must at least meet the parties. Attorney James and I fetched our clients, deciding that if we stayed out, the meeting would be shorter. We hoped Joanne would just say, "Couples do best who mediate, rather than litigate." Mary Ann and Vin emerged after 10 minutes, neither making eye contact. Mary Ann's lips were tightly compressed as she strode quickly toward me. I asked her if she was ready to go upstairs and if she had learned anything from the meeting with Joanne.

"No. He just lies. Anita, I cannot believe he's doing this to the boys. They're such good kids. I told him the boys and I still want him to come home, that we all want him back and please to think of us, not just himself."

We were slotted in the first session with Judge Q. I said, "Mary Ann, we were fortunate to draw Judge Q. She's an attentive, fair, and very able Family Court judge."

As I gave the papers to Michael, the court clerk sitting below the judge, I asked him if he thought we would get in before lunch. He said, "There's one case ahead of you, so I do not know. She usually goes off the bench right at 1:00."

The case being argued finished. The court clerk called the next case, "Jones vs. Jones." No one stood up. This unexpected gap in the list and getting the best judge seemed like the only good luck of the morning. Michael, without really giving enough time for the Joneses to re-enter the courtroom, called out Vin and Mary Ann's last name. We were on a roll if this case could have such a thing as "momentum."

Judge Q. said, "Good morning, Attorney Robboy and Attorney James. I guess I should have said good afternoon! Please identify yourselves for the record and begin with counsel for the moving party. Give me a minute to look at the parties' financial statements, then I will hear from you, Attorney Robboy."

When the judge looked up, I began to speak. "Good afternoon, your honor. May it please the court, I am Anita W. Robboy, and I represent Mary Ann _____, who has been the wife of ..." and I again recited all the basic facts, stressing the long-term nature of the marriage, the joint purchase of the Green Valley Condo, the enormous carrying costs, the ages of the boys, the fact that they were only temporarily away at college but this is their home, the fluidity of Vin's finances, the marked contrasts between his lifestyle and his reported income, the frugality of my client, and so on. I then went on to the most critical aspect of my argument, the level and kind of support I was looking for the judge to order.

"Your honor, I am requesting that this court enter an order requiring Mr. Vin _____ to pay that which he would have paid had he not left his family, namely the mortgage, the condo fees, the utilities, and, in addition, the sum of $400 per week. I propose that half that amount be paid as child support and half as alimony. I have prepared a proposed order in accordance with my request. I recognize that Mr. _____ will argue that he has insufficient income to meet this obligation, so I propose, your honor, that you order that the parties divide equally at this time the joint bank account listed on the husband's financial statement. It is in the amount of $10,000. Permit either side to use these funds as they see fit. The bank account, after division, will be a separate asset of each party, not subject to further equitable distribution.

"I have also, on behalf of my client, filed a motion for counsel fees. I would ask your honor to order an amount of counsel fees identical to that which the husband has paid to his attorney. My client should not be disadvantaged further than she already is by lack of comparable funds to proceed in this matter not of her choosing."

Judge Q. nodded, then said, "Attorney James, I will hear from you."

Attorney James acknowledged that I had recited the facts accurately and then said, "I would only add that my client has funded a large portion of the boys' college education—paying not less than $5,000 since the commencement of the second term, that he has outstanding business loans of $300,000 as listed on Exhibit B, that he also has no discretionary money, that the parties need to ready the property for sale, and that the proposed order is at best only a stop-gap solution to the parties' dire financial circumstances. I propose that the court order support in the amount of 40 percent of my client's gross weekly income as reflected on line 1(a) of the financial statement, a draw of $500 per week. The draw actually is in an amount that exceeds the present profitability of the newly formed company, and it may well have to be adjusted downward in the ensuing months. We propose that my client pay the weekly support sum of $200 per week for the family, ear-marking all of it as alimony as my client has paid so much toward the college expenses, and that neither party be obligated to pay the mortgage or condo fees.

"As far as Attorney Robboy's request for counsel fees, I also have not been paid. In fact, Mr. _____ owes my firm monies for past services rendered to his newly formed company which we are still waiting to receive."

Attorney James handed the Judge his proposed order. Judge Q. then looked at the clients and asked each of them if they would like to say anything. Mary Ann said, "Yes."

The judge smiled and said, "I will hear from you first," then, looking at Vin, said, "You will have an opportunity to speak, so please do not interrupt your wife, as then I cannot hear what is being said."

Mary Ann said, "I have told Vin he is welcome to come home. The boys and I want him to come back. It is very hard without him and—" She began to weep. "I still love him and just do not understand how he can leave us and do this to the boys."

Judge Q. then said, "Mr. _____, would you like to speak?"

"Yes," Vin said. "I am doing my very best to make a success of the copying business. My partner and I have been putting in 80-hour weeks, and I wish that I had the money to pay for the condo, but it just is not there. I would ask that you enter an order that I can meet, as I am trying to keep the boys in college and make payroll expenses."

Judge Q. thanked the clients, Attorney James, and me and concluded as she rose by saying, "I will take the matter under advisement, and you will receive the order in the mail." The court clerk declared, "All rise. The court is now in recess until 2:00 P.M."

Mary Ann immediately asked me, "What happens now? What am I supposed to do? The mortgage is due the first of the month and the grace period is over tomorrow and …."

Her sentence trailed off, and her unanswered questions reverberated in my head as she suddenly ran to catch Vin and Attorney James, almost through the courtroom doorway. I heard her despairing and beseeching words, in a voice far too loud for the silence of a vacating courtroom, "How can you do this to me and the boys?"

Vin walked on out of the courtroom without response. I caught up reluctantly with Mary Ann at the threshold and said, "I will call you the minute I receive anything in the mail. Judge Q. is efficient, and I would not be surprised if she mailed her order within the week. I know she heard the need for prompt attention to your case."

It was raining as I walked to my car, happy to be released from the company and pain of Mary Ann. I did not feel good about this case but consoled myself with the thought that I was not too bad in my presentation to Judge Q. I had told Mary Ann that the judge probably would not decide from the bench. The more hotly a case is argued, the less likely a judge will give his or her judgment from the bench, as that only produces further argument from the lawyers. I knew that Mary Ann was disappointed and scared, which I could well understand. She had been warned that the court process was not a panacea, that judges do not act quickly, and how she had fared would remain a mystery for over two weeks.

By the time the result arrived, Mary Ann had arranged to borrow funds from her parents to meet that month's mortgage payment. The order required Vin to pay the mortgage and pay $200 per week in support for Mary Ann and the children. The joint bank account was to be divided equally. There was no reference to payment of college costs and expenses—or to Mary Ann's legal fees.

Sheila's Motion to Vacate

In the scenarios in this book, there was no reported history of physical abuse or violence. Only when physical violence occurs in the childless, short marriage or a childless protectorate marriage is leaving the situation relatively simple. Complications multiply when there are children of the marriage or when a battered spouse has lost perspective on what a healthy marriage might be like.

Sheila came to me a day after an intense argument, accompanied by blows from her husband, Stephen, the father of her two children, ages five and three. She did not know what to do. He had stormed out of the house, and she had not heard from him since. A former client of mine, a dear friend of Sheila's, had given her my name. Sheila called and said it was terribly important that we meet immediately. I listened to her version of the fight and asked her if she was worried for her safety. She said she was, especially since it was not the first instance of violence in their marriage but one of many. She admitted that the beatings had grown more violent and frequent in the last months. Stephen was a drinker. Sheila said she also was "into the liquor" but had been better since Christmas.

I asked Sheila if she was prepared to seek a divorce or if she was only hoping to get some space. I explained that not all temporary orders are filed in connection with a pending divorce; they may be filed as a result of a complaint for separation. She said she thought that might suit her better; she was not sure of anything today except that she was afraid. If Stephen could change, she did not want to leave him.

We prepared an affidavit in support of the motion to vacate, setting forth the facts and circumstances of the marriage, the arguments, and the ensuing physical violence. It concluded that Sheila was in fear for her and her children's safety and welfare. She also feared that there was a substantial likelihood that if Stephen remained in the home there would be further violence. In addition to the motion to vacate, we prepared a protective order that required Stephen to stay away from the home and not contact Sheila or the children. The order, if entered, carried criminal sanctions. I arranged to present the matter as an emergency motion. Unlike Mary Ann's matter, the same judge allowed the motion on the day of hearing, provided that it would be reheard in three days, at which point the judge would hear from both parties. I was to have the judge's order delivered to Stephen in person by a sheriff.

A motion to vacate, combined with a protective order, is a powerful weapon: It results in someone being thrown out of his or her home, with no chance to argue the fairness of the motion until after the judge has ruled. In addition, all contact between the alleged abuser and his or her family ends, pending further hearing. Though temporary in nature, a motion to vacate should not be used lightly. Even when it is justified, its usage causes tremendous ill will, marking the case for its duration and coloring the parties' relationship for the rest of their lives.

Sheila's dilemma was grave. Either course of action was fraught with peril. Many battered women avoid a motion to vacate for this very reason. Battered women often accept their man's apologies and promises to reform rather than testify about the abuse and live with the wrath of a person who has been evicted from the home.

How a case is handled at the temporary order stage makes a difference in the quality of the parties' aftermarriage. Short-term gains may prove costly: Everything that goes around comes around, especially with separating spouses. Divorcing people need to remember that the time spent in the process is a mere blip compared to the long relationship of aftermarriage. Temporary orders are often a stark reminder that complete satisfaction with the ultimate result, compared to the standard of living they enjoyed during the intact marriage, is an unrealistic and unrealizable goal.

CHAPTER 11

Financial Disclosure

The process of acquiring financial information is called discovery. The financial story of the marriage is learned through the words and documents of the parties, of business colleagues, of family and financial experts who know the parties or can evaluate their assets and income.

Whether mediation, negotiation, or litigation is the chosen divorce process, the financial statement is the heart of any divorce case. It sets forth the assets, liabilities, and income of each party. In the last decade, the lawyer's involvement has been increasingly called for in its preparation. Not only does the client sign the document under pains and penalties of perjury, but the attorney must also certify its accuracy.

Preparing a complete and accurate financial statement may be a daunting task for the client as well as for counsel. Even well-intentioned clients can and do make mistakes. Omitted bank accounts are very problematic unless the interest is listed on the tax returns. Omitted real estate presents the same kind of problem. Valuables not itemized on insurance schedules are not likely to be traceable in the presented paperwork. I wonder whether the high standards imposed on attorneys are fair in light of the realities of the situation. On the other hand, a "fair" financial settlement can only be reached or judgment rendered if all parties and the court have access to complete financial information about all marital assets, income, and liabilities.

Sometimes the asset or income stream is elusive or murky. The occasional extra job, the sporadic royalty check, the cash business, the unvested stock option, the remote future vested interest of a beneficiary of a trust outside of the country are all examples of slippery financial issues. Further complicating matters, divorcing couples often relocate and cannot accurately estimate the expenses (such as heat, water, maintenance, and repair) of the new dwelling. The degree of certainty of each entry on the financial statement must be noted. Entries may be "anticipated" and/or "estimated" or "actual." These labels must be handled with care. The financial statement is a monumentally important document, as are the schedules that are attached to the document for clarification purposes.

The certification requirement imposed on attorneys creates yet greater need for vigilance. A client's error is no defense to a misleading or false financial statement. The new rules regarding counsel's responsibility for accurate financial disclosure are extremely significant. I, as every attorney who practices in this area of the law, must investigate my client's financial circumstances with increased care and suspicion. Has the client accurately stated all of his or her income and assets? It behooves me to check each and every entry. I must not rely blindly on my client. I must request that every client bring in the back-up information so that I can monitor the correctness of each entry. Over time, I have become increasingly wary in my relationships with clients. I am vouching for their honesty and ability to represent accurately their financial circumstances without any power to control their secret conduct. Vin's attorney may have done his best to produce all the evidence he was given. He may well have sought verification from the accountant as Mary Ann did, but the person who really controlled what escaped into the public arena was ultimately Vin. If Vin arranged his business affairs elusively and without any paper trail, he retained a great deal of financial power, at least in the short term.

The dishonorable client can appear in many guises and forms. Social class, intelligence, wit, and charm play on my prejudices but do not assure financial integrity. The dishonest client is a danger to himself, as well as to me. Intentional dishonesty, even conduct merely bordering on furtive behavior, is treated harshly by the judicial system. Credibility of a party/witness is always central to the result. Misstatements of assets and/or income that are substantial, intentional, or for the purpose of misleading the court, are handled punitively. Even unintentional mistakes or errors in the financial statement soil a party's credibility. The financial statement is the paramount document of any divorce case, and it must be handled with the greatest of care.

While I need to believe my client's emotional story unquestioningly, I must adopt a different attitude toward the financial story. The financial story becomes credible only after I have examined the statements and underlying documents of a financial statement for myself. My client is no more to be trusted in terms of finances than his or her spouse. I should only trust opposing counsel after I have found his or her word trustworthy. I must approach everything I see, hear, or observe with a ruthless detachment and cynicism. While I may desire to trust and honor the truth of another person's financial statements, it is a luxury that I cannot afford. I feel deeply ambivalent about the attitude I have unintentionally and involuntarily adopted after years of practicing as a family law attorney. Maybe family law is more fraught with the need to distrust one's own client than many other areas of the law. The necessity of approaching all clients with wariness rather than a trusting posture is a harsh, painful lesson, but the effective practice of law demands it.

Discovering the Financial Facts

The discovery process was designed to be self-executing. The underlying concept was that lawyers would voluntarily exchange all relevant documents without the necessity of court supervision. One side would merely request from the other side, with the proper formalities, any and all relevant information. Each side would behave in good faith by responding in a timely fashion and by producing all requested material; neither side would hide material information. After the lawyers had gathered and exchanged all the relevant information, the court's focus, time, and energy could exclusively be applied to deciding the substance of the case. Efficiency would be served by eliminating surprise evidence at trial.

That was the intent. This is the reality. There are many well-known examples of the failure of discovery to be self-executing, of the lofty concept of full and timely disclosure gone awry. Both former President Clinton and former President Nixon's responses to discovery are examples of "stonewalling" the process. Their lawyers did not voluntarily provide the documents requested and did not foster a climate of open exchange of information with the purpose of facilitating the discovery of all relevant information. Their conduct was counterproductive, misleading, and, at best, marginally responsive.

There is no question that extracting all relevant information from one's own client can be cumbersome and time-consuming. However, it is critical to a successful process. Some family law attorneys simply do not bother, instead focusing on creating obstacles to the other side's obtaining all relevant information. Such discovery games create an enormous amount of extra work for opposing counsel and increase the expense and frustration of the divorce process.

The system is built on the assumption that the attorney for each side will voluntarily provide to the other side all relevant information. Regardless of a client's reluctance to disclose all, even to his or her own attorney, let alone to the opposing side, attorneys are regulated by a code of ethics that demands honest compliance with this process. The ethos of many attorneys is to make the process as difficult and expensive as possible for their opponent. Instead of facilitating the flow of information, some attorneys view their task as protecting sensitive materials from ever being disclosed or for as long as possible. Some aim to cooperate only to the minimum extent necessary. In these instances, the goal of exchanging information for purposes of narrowing and clarifying the issues for trial is lost entirely. The focus is on turning the discovery process into a contest. Both clients pay dearly for this.

Many divorcing people find the discovery process a nightmare. Even where both spouses proceed in good faith, the expense of obtaining an appraisal of a family business, a complex real estate interest, or a retirement and stock option plan can be staggering. Not infrequently, the spouses do not know the value of their assets, and, therefore, third persons such as appraisers, business evaluators, accountants, keepers of the records, or plan administrators must be called upon, adding to the cost of the divorce. The discovery process can be an even worse nightmare when anyone involved fails to be financially forthcoming, truthful, accurate, and complete. That person might be one's own client, the spouse of the client, the opposing lawyer, or a witness.

Divorcing spouses frequently experience intense frustration and anger at the seeming lack of full and honest compliance with requests for information. The same spouses may have a different but equally intense emotional reaction to requests for their own financial information. His, or her, feelings often center around a sense of outrage at the breadth and depth of the discovery sought, the invasion of privacy, and what can seem like the witch hunt quality of the process. The scope of permissible discovery is very, very broad. Every shred of documentary evidence may be requested, including bank accounts, cancelled checks, credit card information, loan applications, stock brokerage statements, diaries or calendars, professional and personal correspondence, to name but a few of the possibilities. The process can feel like an extended invasion of the client's boundaries, privacy, and dignity. Few clients actually enjoy watching their spouse sweat, squirm, or seek to evade the truth. Attorneys also have reason to fear the discovery process since failure to do proper discovery exposes them to malpractice suits.

The story that follows illustrates a divorcing person's distressing and expensive discovery experience. It also illustrates the difficulties that lawyers face when the discovery process does not operate in the proper way.

Mary Ann's Discovery Nightmare

Mary Ann, long married to Vin, needed information about Vin's Kwik Copy business in order to assess his true financial circumstances. Mary Ann, like many wives in classic marriage bargains, had very incomplete knowledge of Vin's finances. She had been the partner more responsible for homemaking, and Vin had been the primary breadwinner of the family. The couple had appeared once in Family Court for the purpose of a temporary support order and counsel fees. They had exchanged financial statements at that time, but Mary Ann knew that Vin had failed to be truthful about his finances. He had to have made more money than he confessed to, and he surely had more assets than he had listed. His Kwik Copy business had not been assigned any value, an omission that Mary Ann knew was nonsense.

The parties were to exchange financial documentation and information pursuant to a form known as a Production of Documents. Vin's counsel, Attorney James, ignored the request. Attorney James ignored Mary Ann's request for a revised, complete, up-to-date financial statement and request for documents relating to Vin's business. Belatedly, and long after both kinds of documents were due, Vin and his counsel responded to Mary Ann's Production of Documents Request with responses such as, "not in plaintiff's custody, possession, or control," "not relevant" and the proverbial, "to be produced." The financial statement, the most essential document of them all, was among the documents, "to be produced." The net result of the request in terms of real information was paltry, only a thin folder of relevant and irrelevant documents. A written and oral request to Attorney James reiterating the request (and even explaining the relevance of the requested documents) proved fruitless. Mary Ann was left with the choice of: seeking the documents from sources other than her spouse, returning to court for judicial assistance, engaging in more discovery, and then seeking judicial help, or giving up the struggle.

Based on my experience with the court's attitude toward discovery, I advised Mary Ann that a judge might well not respond sympathetically to her plight unless she could show that she had exhausted all other reasonable sources of obtaining the requested information.

The first place to seek business information from an uncooperative spouse engaged in business is his keeper of the records of the business. As Mary Ann knew, that person was none other than Jill, whom Vin saw day and night. She could have handed to Vin the records kept in the ordinary course of business without any discovery fanfare, had Vin chosen to make the process self-executing. Instead, the notice of deposition would have to be sent to the main office of the business, and Jill would have to appear in her official capacity with the documents in my office. My fees to do this work would be charged to Mary Ann, a person who hated every part of her situation and now had one more unseemly part to abhor, paying me to get documents from Jill.

After additional psychic pain, time, aggravation, and expense, the payroll records and some other data appeared. However, the business tax returns were not in the "custody, possession, or control" of the keeper of the records. They could only be obtained from the accountant of the newly formed business, at the expense of my client, a struggling school teacher. Mary Ann's legal bill already exceeded her limited ability to pay and the case had hardly begun.

My nightmare also had started. My worries were caused by insufficient information to assess the financial picture fully, limited funds to ferret out additional information, obstreperous conduct from the other side, and an inability to withdraw without Mary Ann's having found an attorney to take my place. As Mary Ann had no slush funds, either for herself or for hiring new counsel, I doubted that I would be rescued from the situation. Vin's business had to be appraised, and the court had not granted her either counsel fees or expert fees in the case. Mary Ann's financial resources were tapped out, as she and I knew all too well. Yet adequate trial preparation necessitated that she borrow funds for an appraisal; she could not allow Vin to get away with assigning his business no value whatsoever.

The deposition of Vin's accountant produced no satisfaction because Vin's business tax returns were "on extension" and last year's had yet to be filed. Vin's accountant was working on the late tax returns but was stymied by Vin's failure to produce the relevant information that would enable the accountant to complete the returns.

Thus far, I had made all the right moves but still had exposure for failing to obtain necessary information. I knew that Vin's numbers would be unreliable as Mary Ann had given me ample reason to suspect his credibility, and I had an incomplete set of documents from which to draw financial conclusions.

My situation, like my client's, is horribly uncomfortable. I am held to a high standard of care and diligence in defending Mary Ann. I must make sure that she has accurate and complete financial information before advising her to accept any proposed divorce settlement. Yet how can I advise her adequately when the other side is making it so difficult and the resources are so limited? Vin may not be intentionally malevolent, but from Mary Ann's perspective, he is throwing up a smoke screen around the marital assets, and there is no way to penetrate smoke. I know that I will be judged at a later time as if I had the resources at hand, certainly with respect to the value of the business. Lawyers need to practice defensively, but doing so in this kind of a case is enormously challenging. As Mary Ann's counsel, I must insist on further court appearances to show that I left no stone unturned in my diligent hunt for financial information. Mary Ann may not have wanted so many court appearances as now are likely to be scheduled, but I am invested in protecting my law license by a showing of zealous pursuit of the truth.

Judicial Attitude

Courts dislike hearing discovery squabbles, as the system was designed to be self-executing. The judicial attitude is that the attorneys have failed when the system does not operate smoothly. There is a great deal of truth in this conclusion, but not all the participants are necessarily equally responsible for this unfortunate result. If the opposing party fails to comply, the other side may take the issue of noncompliance before the court. The side seeking compliance may file a motion for an order seeking compliance, as well as sanctions in the form of attorneys fees, or request that the judge appoint a Special Master to assist in the discovery process. (Such person is known as a Discovery Master.)

Not following the rules can take many forms and happens wittingly or unwittingly. The discovery can be made unfairly onerous by a party not complying with the time frames, not answering questions asked, not answering questions completely, or failing to provide the specific information sought. Yet most courts do not really want to hear the details of how and why discovery has gone badly awry. "A pox on all of you" is all too often the judicial stance. The situation is unfortunate from every perspective, including the couple's aftermarriage relationship.

However, not every person behaves as Vin and his counsel did. The following case illustrates a refreshingly cooperative and open spirit of the participants and counsel, an ideal enactment of the discovery concept at its best.

Henry and Eleanor: Exchange of Financial Information

Henry and Eleanor, another classic marriage bargain couple, proceeded very differently through discovery. Admittedly, it was far easier, since the marital assets were simply the home and Henry's salary, consulting income, investment income, royalty income, and retirement benefits. It was also easier because the couple shared genuine good faith and financial power politics had played no part in their marriage or separation.

Neither side questioned the other's financial integrity. Henry scrupulously kept all the slips, documents, and correspondence relating to his extra income. Eleanor was a thorough record keeper and managed the family's finances. Only the attorneys' desire to safeguard against the possible future malpractice action would have required a deposition, a request for production of documents, or interrogatories. Had Eleanor's attorney requested any discovery from the college, Henry would have been mortified. To avoid such an implied questioning of his integrity, Henry went to the personnel department without waiting for any formal notice by Eleanor to the college keeper of records. Another person with another lawyer might have caused unnecessary discomfort to Henry, but Eleanor protected the quality of her aftermarriage by not insisting that documents only be delivered to her by the college's keeper of records. Henry was supremely cooperative, and Eleanor and her counsel appreciated that using "honey" rather than "vinegar" produced the desired result.

Guiding a client through the maze of the discovery process while remembering that only the client and the client's children will reap the consequences of future hostility and ill will from a former spouse calls for a cautious but firm approach. Failure to supply documents is unacceptable, but open warfare is also undesirable. The ideal strategy is to straddle the fine line between making firm requests and using teeth if they are not complied with. Reminding the recalcitrant spouse of the couple's necessary future connections may cause the spouse to be more helpful. Unfortunately, in Vin's case, he was eager to finish his marriage but not eager to produce the necessary documents. He had no agenda to harm Mary Ann, but he also had no inclination to manage his business with her interests in the forefront of his business plans.

How much discovery does a case need? The answer depends on the facts and circumstances. The following story illustrates a sensible amount in light of the couple's financial circumstances.

Bettina and Mark's Finances

In Bettina and Mark's case (the protectorate marital bargain couple), Mark's attorney sought little discovery. He thought it highly unlikely that Bettina had any hidden accounts; she had only a puny income stream from her art, and inquiry was not worth the expense. If the other side has undisclosed bank accounts or a side business that a spouse of many years does not know about, is that information likely to pop up in the requested discovery? The answer is usually "no." For better or worse, a spouse is usually the best detective on the case. Unless the client insists and is willing to pay, my usual attitude is that further discovery is a waste of time and energy.

Mark's income stream was not difficult to assess, but the extent of his interest in the medical practice was not so simple to ascertain. His financial statement reflected no interest in the business, but that may have been an unwitting omission or genuine ignorance. Often clients do not understand the legal interpretation of ownership or interest in an endeavor and mistakenly describe their financial relationship. An attorney must be satisfied of the true nature and value of the business interest. When a party has a privately held business interest, an expert appraisal must be obtained, even at a substantial cost. Not all clients listen as the following case demonstrates.

Zack and Ginny: Unacknowledged Complexity

In the case of Zack and Ginny, the complex marital bargain couple, the complexity was emotional and financial. All complexities were to be carefully contained by a tacit agreement not to acknowledge any complexity. Zack had a diverse financial profile consisting of interests in real-estate ventures, partnerships, limited partnerships, corporations, and one subchapter S Corporation. Ginny did not even know the names of all Zack's business interests, much less have any concrete financial information about them.

Complete verified financial documentation is a bedrock condition of any fair resolution. How could any reasonable agreement be reached without knowing the real values of the marital assets? However, Ginny wanted the case managed in the style of their marriage. She urged Zack to mediate, and he was delighted to accommodate, as he knew that he had exclusive knowledge of the marital finances.

The mediation process has no system to compel a person to tell more about finances than he voluntarily agrees to report. The mediator can ask the couple to fill out their respective financial statements and bring back-up information. There is no right to take depositions, demand answers to interrogatories, or compel the production of documents. A mediator can only suggest that an appraisal of property or a business would be wise, not order one. If both parties do not agree to obtain a valuation of a business interest, then it is unlikely to occur. Ginny wanted no appraisals, so none were obtained. Ginny and Zack's mediated settlement agreement was crafted on the basis of Zack's numbers for his various businesses. While Zack had no agenda to harm Ginny, he preferred keeping his company affairs private and understated. Given Ginny's attitude toward ending her marriage and family finances, mediation was the path of least resistance. Zack preferred no verifiable, rigid scrutiny of his businesses. He was pleased to set the value of his business interests.

Complex financial information demands sophisticated verification processes. Mediation does not lend itself to this unless the parties are sophisticated enough to ask for, and obtain, financial information. A lawyer coach can help couples going through mediation, particularly if they doubt their own financial acumen. A lawyer who coaches a client in mediation does not have the right to file discovery requests unless the client agrees and, even more importantly, unless a court action has been commenced. A court action commences with a pleading, usually called a complaint for divorce or a petition. In mediation, no papers are filed with the court until the parties have reached a full and complete settlement.

Discovery and the Right Divorce Process

In a perfect world, the philosophy of self-executing discovery would operate to ensure that everybody would seamlessly comply with the principles of full disclosure. Unfortunately, the process of undoing an intact marriage is an occasion where people are likely to be motivated to understate their assets and overstate their liabilities. The greatest need for an effective discovery process exists where there is the least trust between the spouses. The need for an effective system to compel valuations is greatest where there are complex assets. Without effective discovery, the nature of the complex asset may only be known incompletely. A divorcing person should assess his or her marital estate and then choose a divorce process that will enable full disclosure in light of the nature of the assets and the nature and good will of his or her spouse.

Divorcing people often come face to face with the awful truth that their spouse, credible and trustworthy in many areas of life, is not so in the financial arena. Financial deviousness may or may not accompany emotional betrayal or emotional disappointments. The shock of learning that the once relied upon provider can call gold "copper" in the context of separation is disarming. The journey to aftermarriage and the trust that may endure thereafter, if any, is very dependent on the spouses treating their finances in the most forthright, complete, and open manner possible. This requirement can be extremely difficult where, and when, the assets and income are fluid and variable because of the nature of their sources. Trust is easier to protect if the parties are wage earners and the assets are held in simple instruments in a consolidated form, all at one bank and with one brokerage house, for example. Divorcing couples should make every effort and appearance of effort to comply with discovery requests. The production of information is not a game that ought to be treated casually or as a "cat and mouse" endeavor but as essential to their future ability to cooperate and communicate. Either ex-spouse may need to rely on the other's goodwill long after the divorce hearing, should unexpected circumstances such as involuntary unemployment, illness, disability, or disaster occur to them or their children. How the parties deal with each other during their disengagement will create a long shadow over the quality of their relationship in aftermarriage.

CHAPTER 12

Making a Deal

A separation or settlement agreement is a document executed by both parties (notarized or witnessed) which defines all past, present, and future rights, duties, and obligations between the spouses. It addresses many issues: custody, child support, alimony, division of real and personal property, debts, health and life insurance, taxes, counsel fees, and the effect/status of the agreement. Reaching a separation agreement (known also as a settlement agreement) means that the couple has avoided a divorce trial. Instead of a full trial, counsel and the parties appear in court for a brief hearing. The presiding judge must find that the parties' settlement agreement is "fair and reasonable," in light of the circumstances. In most states, after the settlement agreement has been approved, there is a waiting period *before* the divorce is *final.*

The settlement process commences with one side's lawyer offering the other side's lawyer a partial or a comprehensive proposal, orally or in writing. The recipient responds with a counter-proposal containing new aspects and the acceptable earlier provisions. This dialogue continues until an acceptable compromise agreement has been reached.

Negotiation is a constant theme. Lawyers try to reach agreement as early as possible on as many issues as possible. Even if the case is going to trial, most lawyers have a draft separation agreement in their trial bag so that if the case settles before or during trial, the lawyers can commit their fresh understandings to writing. The road to trial never precludes the road to settlement, and the two are frequently traveled simultaneously, with settlements often reached the day before or the day of the trial.

The essence of successful negotiation is compromise and flexibility of frames. Civility and a personable style are key ingredients as well. Can the skill be acquired or is it dependent upon one's personality and character? My own experience in practicing law is that one gets better with time, but excellence does not automatically come with experience.

Reasonable attorneys make offers and counter-offers that are within the box of reasonable settlement. The fuzzy areas are clarified and shaped according to the situation. The experienced practitioner can predict what each side will request because he or she has argued both sides of any issue. The chess moves in divorce negotiation are familiar and repetitive. Lawyers know the advantages and disadvantages of staying in the marital home or receiving an early distribution for short money if one represents the departing spouse whose equity would otherwise be tied up in the marital home. What a lawyer chooses to propose in any given case depends upon whom he or she represents. Even more importantly, a lawyer must be sensitive to the magical moments when the divorcing couple are ready to compromise. Reaching settlement calls for letting go of some needs in order to resolve the really important issues. The same dilemmas recur; the same sticking points repeat; and the number of solutions is finite. For instance, the marital home can be kept by the husband, kept by the wife, or sold, now or later. There are no other solutions.

The Settlement Conference

Settlement conferences are often the first time I meet the estranged spouse, whom I have only seen through the eyes of my client. A settlement conference can occur before or after financial information has been exchanged, even before any papers have been filed to begin the divorce process. It may happen before and after a hearing on temporary orders, as attorneys repeatedly try to resolve the issues, with and without judicial assistance. Usually both lawyers and clients are present or on telephone call. Some attorneys prefer to negotiate deals without the client watching, feeling that the meeting may be more productive if neither side is inclined to take a position for appearance's sake. I do not subscribe to this school of thought as I believe that it is even more important to include the client in the negotiation process.

I am always curious to meet and observe my client's spouse. It is one of my private high points in family law practice. The person my client may have described as a bully or beautiful, I may see as a pussycat or plain. I am also curious to watch how the couple relate. Are they behaving like friendly monarchs or sworn enemies? Do they make eye contact? Do they address each other? Are they comfortable in each other's presence? Do they interrupt each other or answer for each other? Do they still act like a married couple?

How they relate tells me a great deal about the future of the case. A couple that demonstrate some care for each other are far more likely to settle their differences amicably than a couple who do not make eye contact or verbally assault each other. When one party still holds on to the illusion that the marriage can be fixed by commitment or will power, rapid settlement is unlikely. However, excessive friendliness, intimacy, or affection in a lawyer's office also sets off warning lights: I worry that my client may not be ready to leave the comfort of an intact marriage.

Interruption and anger between the spouses may be of several types. Constant interruptions or belittling remarks indicate to me a lack of respect and a power imbalance between the spouses. Angry exchanges, however, may indicate a lingering bond. Indifference is the opposite of love, but intense negative feelings may not be. Furious outbursts will be the other side of the love coin and may be a clue that the couple are engaging in a love/hate dance that is far from over. Not every divorce that begins makes it to the finish line! The filing of divorce papers may be an elaborate intervention to make one party stop drinking, a complex ritual of rejection and forgiveness after an affair, or even the result of an undiagnosed depression. The emotional quality of the spouses' communication is a significant indicator of the likelihood of reaching agreement.

Reaching Agreement: Henry and Eleanor (Classic Couple)

Henry, the college professor, and I went to Eleanor's attorney's office for the first settlement conference within a month of my initial meeting with Henry. Eleanor had hired Attorney Christel to represent her, and I was very pleased by her choice, both for Henry's sake and mine. Attorney Christel is very thorough and has high standards for what is a reasonable settlement, particularly when she represents the woman's side. She and I are personal friends, not unusual in the relatively tight family-law bar, which neither Eleanor nor Henry minded when so informed.

After coffee, tea, and water had been offered, the meeting began in earnest. Henry had asked me to speak for him as much as possible; we had decided to follow the "good cop, bad cop" model of negotiating, and I would be the bad one and he would be the good one. Henry and I had prepared for the conference by identifying the box of reasonable settlement and then calculating two offers slightly outside it in two distinct and generous ways. We knew what pieces of the offers were essential, less essential, and disposable. All of us were working with the same financial information, compiled in large part by Eleanor. The only fuzzy asset was the fair market value of the parties' home; two local real-estate brokers had rendered opinions that were $40,000 apart. Henry's salary raises over time could be projected with sufficient accuracy, and Henry had obtained retirement benefit data and medical and life insurance information from the college.

Attorney Christel recognized Henry's offer of settlement as ample, if not magnanimous, and asked for a few significant modifications. Henry, the good guy, spoke up and substantially agreed to Attorney Christel's request. We reached agreement on all the issues in less than two and a half hours. The case was easy to manage because the clients had realistic expectations, complete and rapid financial disclosure, and income and assets that were identifiable and of ascertainable value. The only possible point of contention was the amount of alimony Henry should pay Eleanor and for how long considering both Henry's eventual retirement and the fact that he would not be idle even when he did retire from the college. The agreement fixed alimony at a set amount per year, augmented by an annual cost of living escalator, and an end point upon Henry's sixty-eighth birthday, regardless of his earnings from consulting, teaching, or writing. All retirement assets were split equally, and Eleanor received the house.

Neither party had any rancor toward the other, only a sweet tristesse. As I watched this couple relate with such harmony, dignity, and consideration of each other's feelings, I wondered why they were divorcing. The usual problem areas attributed to the breakdown of marriage are money, power, and sex—all seemingly absent. Was Eleanor responding to a feeling of enormous loneliness, internal restlessness, or incessant yearning for something she did not have? Eleanor's dissatisfaction was not based on betrayal, distrust, or breach of an earlier agreement as existed in the case of the other classic couple, Mary Ann and Vin. I did not imagine Eleanor to be any more isolated from Henry at this time than she had been earlier in the marriage. Would she say, if asked, that only now has she awakened to her true circumstances?

My impression as I watched this couple's passage to after-marriage is that Eleanor did not sufficiently value the force, power, and magnitude of their common history. She and, consequently, they were trading known connections for distance and even further isolation. I wonder if Eleanor is railing against an internalized promise she received somewhere years earlier that in love, marriage, and family life she would discover complete fulfillment. Henry also offers no clues to his deepest feelings; he and I talk classics, or rather I listen and learn about classics, rather than dwelling on breaches of classic marriage bargains.

Wheeling and Dealing

Every divorce case will require trade-offs, so it is essential to know what is nonnegotiable, negotiable, and of no significance to both sides. The calculation must be made not only for the side one represents but also from the perspective of the other side. The major breadwinner may be willing to trade a higher starting level of support, even a guaranteed amount regardless of decreases or increases in his income, in exchange for the freedom to earn larger amounts in the future. He may also be willing to waive any right to seek a reduction in support if his ex-wife goes back to work. He prefers to know his obligation and protect himself from a former spouse looking in his pocket in later years. The wife in this example may be concerned that she always be able to live in the former marital residence and not have to go to work in order to do so. Henry and Eleanor made just this sort of trade-off, with a few extra details. Other couples may not want to take such a gamble on their future job security. These couples want to ride with the actual facts and not have what may turn into a draconian support order in case there is a downturn in the market.

Many cases stumble on what to do upon retirement. Should the issue be left open? When I represent the provider, I am concerned that leaving the issue open will give the ex-spouse future rights to seek the same or higher alimony upon retirement, especially if the provider frugally saves money between divorce and retirement. When I represent the dependent spouse, I am concerned that such spouse not be left unprotected after the provider retires. She may never manage to create a retirement fund from her present level of support, and her earning capacity may be marginal or unknown, so she will want to keep the issue of post-retirement support alive at all costs. The compromise may be that the provider will never have to pay more than X dollars nor less than Y dollars for Z years.

A good strategy in negotiating is to target some aspect of the bargain as "highly important," but know in one's heart that it could be surrendered. In other words, it may be wise to inflate the value of certain chits so that one appears to be making a great concession, even if it is not true. Each side wants to feel that he or she got an "extra." It is the same mentality any store uses in tagging an item as specially discounted. We all like to feel that we got a bargain.

Regardless of one's true assessment, it is important to behave as if the other side got the better deal and point out the pain caused by each trade-off. Flattery may also be a powerful weapon, and its timely usage can often smooth the negotiation process.

In addition to these well-worn strategies, one should negotiate with an eye to the clock. The time value of money or any promise is extremely important. If the sum offered upon reflection seems high, the true cost can be greatly reduced by paying the same amount over time. Conversely, if my client's spouse is in need of immediate cash, she or he may accept less money if paid rapidly. Timing of needs is a critical calculation. Often a husband will accept short money for his interest in the marital home in exchange for receiving the equity before the children reach the age of emancipation because he wants the cash to make a down payment on a new residence or business purchase. The husband may also want the wife to remortgage the house and remove his name. If he accepts the lesser amount, the wife may be able to do both. In addition to receiving the money early and clearing his name, the husband has created future tax savings for himself and transferred the future capital-gains tax liability to the wife. The wife may like this trade-off as she has purchased the husband's one-half interest in the home for a pittance in comparison to its present fair market value. Had the parties not made the trade, the house would have been divided equally only after the youngest child reached the age of majority or finished college. Neither one of them would have reaped the benefits yielded by cooperation.

Sometimes the spread between the offers of settlement can be mended by paying that amount to, or for, the benefit of the parties' children. Many a divorcing parent will willingly contribute money for his or her child's education, especially if the alternate recipient is a former spouse.

The Art of the Deal

Despite the attorneys' best efforts and tactics, some negotiations just go on and on. There is the appearance of serious attempts to settle, but when push comes to shove, the deal slips away. One side gives and gives, and somehow the offer is never enough. Whenever I observe this pattern, I realize it is not about money; it is about something else—emotional torture, perhaps. What appears to be at issue may have nothing to do with the actual conflict in emotional terms. Parties are always settling a myriad of scores while reaching accord.

It is enormously helpful if a couple has insight into their own behaviors. They can then concentrate on the practical aspects of the trade. I find that clients need frequent reminders that the part of their marriage's dissolution *that they are here to discuss* is the dissolution of a financial partnership. It is simultaneously, of course, an enormously complex and intensely emotional journey, but the legal solutions do not and cannot address the emotional turmoil. When the agendas get confused, the parties will pay the price in higher legal fees, further emotional battering, and heartache.

In one case, a deal involving several million dollars nearly failed because the parties could not agree on the fate of a Tiffany chandelier. The husband described how he had gotten it while still in college, long before he knew his wife. The wife responded that it matched the dining room table, which she was entitled to keep. "And besides, I'm moving into a home, and you're going to your *girlfriend's* home, which is *furnished.*" All of the couple's intense pain at letting go of their marriage had attached itself to this one item. They bickered while the other attorney and I listened until one of us finally asked the value of the Tiffany chandelier. It was substantial for a chandelier but not considering their combined wealth. The other lawyer and I suggested that the party who gave up the Tiffany chandelier be paid more than its replacement value. The dispute finally fizzled when one spouse reminded the other that the "Tiffany" lamp was a fake.

Negotiations over personal property can produce a lot of heat. The final task in a difficult, lengthy case comes with the division of household property. Divorce lawyers refer to this part of any case as the "pots and pans," and they try to avoid it like the plague. It usually represents a tiny portion of the marital estate's value, but it is heavily freighted with emotional baggage. For example, one family had three sets of silver cutlery. Lest either party receive a complete set or more than the other, the only agreement that both parties would ultimately accept, after three and a half hours of heated arguing, was each spouse receiving half the knives, forks, and spoons from each set. They considered this resolution fair, as it was absolutely equal; the fact that neither spouse could serve a large dinner gathering with matching silverware was secondary. Each couple comes to the table with their own sense of "fair" trades, and I have learned that the client's notion of fair is much more important than mine, even if I am more sensible!

Secret Bonds

Parties going through a divorce have their own rules about what secrets should, and should not, be kept, even as they march toward dissolution. The following examples illustrate some of the kinds of personal secrets that an otherwise honest client may wish *not to disclose* in negotiations or at trial.

Sometimes an abused spouse will specifically request that her husband's physical or emotional abuse not be used as a bargaining chip in making a deal. "I do not want to talk about that part of our marriage," she may say of her desire to protect her husband. A husband whose wife suffered abuse as a child may also feel this is her secret. I have seen a husband make this choice even if his custody claim at trial might have been strengthened by demonstrating dysfunction in his wife's family. Legitimacy of a child is yet another example of a spousal secret that, like Pandora's box, may never be opened for fear of what might emerge.

Family secrets take many forms. There are secrets that maintain the myth of marriage, of family origin, of individual origin, of a special allegiance or bond between particular family members and between the spouses. Some "dirty" family secrets, such as tax evasion and drug use, are told to attorneys with the specific caveat that they not be revealed. Cases that contain these types of secrets are best ended by a negotiated settlement agreement, rather than litigated. A presiding Family Court judge is a mandated reporter of tax evasion or fraud.

In contrast to certain "dirty" secrets, most other financial secrets are revealed in the public courtroom at trial with a kind of wanton abandon in hopes of being found the holier spouse. A few individual, spousal, and family secrets may never see the light of day, even if it might be advantageous to one of the parties. These few secrets live on even as the parties reach a negotiated settlement agreement or declare that they are telling the whole truth and nothing but the truth. There are some secrets that are too private and/or too painful to ever unearth to anyone outside the family, even as the family is ripped asunder and travel toward the land of aftermarriage.

Settling into Aftermarriage

Many spouses can only psychologically separate after a fight, or with time, or not at all. Settlement agreements, particularly mediated ones, obviate the "fight" and leave the couple to work out their separation over time. One person may never really "separate," and often neither one does, despite all appearances to the contrary. I suspect that all the couples I have described would identify with some aspect of the Ingmar Bergman film *Scenes of a Marriage*. In the last scene, a middle-aged, formerly married couple meet again, each having married someone else, and wonder why they were not able to stay together. I see couples caught in the web of caring and withdrawing, caring and withdrawing, on a daily basis. I watch and try to guide as people get beyond this internal struggle.

Couples who manage to settle rather than litigate the rearrangement of their marriage have demonstrated that they truly care about their relationship and want to conserve emotional and monetary capital for their future in the land of aftermarriage. Honoring the future interests of aftermarriage as well as the current ones in the dissolution of their marriage is the highest expression of civilized behavior during the searing process of redesigning a new contract for aftermarriage.

The story of distancing with continuing intimacy in a new form is often evident in microcosm when a couple parts after an uncontested divorce hearing. Some couples say nothing to each other. Others will kiss and hug. Some cry or have even brought flowers for their former spouse. Others will shake hands and wish each other good luck. Many will offer the other a lift or the chance to sip a cup of coffee together. Some will utter an unrelated reminder, such as, "You're picking up the kids after school, right?" or "Did you take care of the insurance payment?" How the parties part is a preview of how they are entering the land of aftermarriage.

CHAPTER 13

A Judgment Is Only
a Judgment

As a very wise family court judge used to say, "My father was a tailor. He used to tell his customers that if they just wanted a suit, and did not care if it was tailored to their particular and unique measurements, they should just buy one off the rack. If they wanted the suit to fit perfectly, then they should buy one from him. A court ordered judgment of divorce is a suit off the rack."

A mediated agreement, or a negotiated settlement composed by two able attorneys who have their clients' interests and needs in mind, is a tailor-made product. Why is a judgment not of the same quality? No judge can know the clients or their problems as well as the mediator or the attorneys who have had an opportunity to listen over a much longer period of time. A judge meets the clients for the first time on the first day of trial. Even if the parties have been before the judge at the temporary order stage, it would be unusual for the judge to remember the parties, much less the facts. At every court appearance, the parties and their counsel must assume the judge has no prior knowledge.

In contrast, a mediator or the attorneys know the facts intimately and understand the priorities, interests, and concerns of the two parties since they have spent a great deal of time with these people at each stage of the developing tale of divorce.

Not only do the attorneys have a greater familiarity with the case than the judge, but they are also able to offer more varied and more complex and far-reaching solutions for parties in their aftermarriage. The judge will deliver a judgment to the parties that, by its nature and form, provides only a limited range of solutions to a given set of problems. Judgments, like suits off the rack, are manufactured in large quantities in preset sizes of given measurements conforming to the permitted form of judgment, permitted subject matter, and permitted remedies.

The Nature of a Judgment

A judgment is like a snapshot. It captures the scene as it appears at any given moment only. It cannot make provisions for future events which are not certain to occur, however likely they may be. This can be a major problem as very little is static in the lives of a family, regardless of whether or not the parents are cohabiting. A mother may not be working at the time of trial because she has small children. She may hope to become employed in the future when her childcare obligations lessen. Since it is only an expectation at the time of trial, her future earning capacity will not be incorporated into the judgment. Similarly, both parties may expect that their children will attend college. However, a judge would not make college tuition provisions for children as young as Michael and Nicole since college entrance is at least eight years away. Someone might remarry; someone else might land a new and much more lucrative job. The judgment, however, must rest on present and certain facts, not probabilities or reasonable expectations.

A divorce judgment sets the level of appropriate support based on the present financial circumstances of the parties. What might or should happen upon retirement of either party is left until the time is closer and the matter ripe for decision. Had

Henry and Eleanor not entered into a separation agreement, the court's decision would not have addressed Henry's career after the time he retired from college teaching. Mark might have been required to pay to Bettina alimony until a set date when the matter could be reviewed and the level reconsidered in light of Bettina's actual employment and health. A judge would not make an order based on a job she might get, although he might order her to seek employment and impute income to her at a low level.

A Judgment Is Not an Agreement

A separation agreement can "provide for" something or "not provide for" something because the parties want matters handled that way. An agreement designed by the parties can cover circumstances likely to occur in the future whether or not there exists a factual basis for so doing or a legal fiction to justify the action. For example, future educational expenses of the children can be allocated or current money set aside for this future expectation. An agreement can regulate what will happen upon a party's acquisition or loss of employment, increase or decrease in earnings. Parties can choose to commit each other to refinance existing debt such as the mortgage, consolidate credit card debt, file (or amend) joint income tax returns, engage in tax planning strategies when dividing assets, and arrange to share an asset of the marriage.

More importantly, parents can craft unique, harmonious, and compatible child-sharing schedules. They can design a schedule wherein the children (or the parents) rotate their primary residence weekly, monthly, or yearly. The parents can create times when all or some of the children are staying in one home, thereby ensuring quality time with each child. Special activities and interests, tutoring, trips, and summer camp can be bargained for and allocated as an expense of either or both parents in a specially tailored agreement.

The judge would not, and could not, mandate these important extras because they are not strictly defined as child support. The judge follows conventional ways of dealing with children whose parents reside in two separate homes. Children should be kept as a unit and the parental sharing clear and predictable, meaning that the schedule should be the same week in and week out. The visitation schedule will be one that has been entered before and is standard. The judgment will not anticipate the changed needs of children as they grow; the particular schedule of any one member of the family is less important than an overall plan or scheme that can be reviewed for its reasonableness and its enforceability. Flexibility and accommodation between spouses may be desirable, especially around missed visits, but such conduct cannot be prescribed or readily monitored in a judgment and, therefore, is avoided.

Parties can agree to share a vacation home that neither wants to relinquish to the other or cease using. A judge would be very unlikely to write a judgment that leaves the parties intertwined in this way. A spouse may wish to retain an interest in the other spouse's business or at least retain the unexercised stock options or continue to receive the future pension or perks of a particular business. The possibilities for advantageous continued connections are numerous, and an agreement can balance them against the disadvantages of continued involvement. The court is focused on separating the divorcing couple. A judge will only allow parties to continue to own the marital residence jointly where there are minor children for whom stability and continuity of housing are paramount considerations.

In a separation agreement, the divorcing couple can set the distance that they want to stand away from the court system. A separation agreement is incorporated into the judgment of divorce. The parties can choose to have their agreement either "survive" as an independent contract or have the agreement be "merged" in the judgment of divorce. However, certain provisions of the agreement must be either one way or the other. Child-related issues must be merged in the judgment of divorce, and property division provisions must survive. All other provisions of a separation agreement can go either way. Where parties want to make their agreement survive as an independent contract, they have, in effect, asked the court never to change their deal unless there are extreme and compelling circumstances that were not foreseen by the parties at the time they entered into their agreement. By contrast, a merged separation agreement can be more readily modified at a later time upon the showing of a substantial change of circumstances. Parties who value finality are better served by a separation agreement that is not merged into a court judgment but has independent legal significance. Parties who value future flexibility are wise to elect a merged separation agreement.

Historically, judgments are almost always entered on the narrowest possible grounds. Thus, a judge will decide on a procedural ground only, if possible, and avoid addressing the substance of the litigation. If there are no procedural grounds upon which to dispose of a case, then and only then, will the judge focus on "the merits," or subject matter, the part that means the most to the litigants of a case. When deciding a case on the merits, the presiding judge will once again seek the narrowest basis for decision. In the area of divorce litigation, the narrowest basis usually means only the immediate situation.

Every judgment is the basis for future judgments, a principle known in the law as "*stare decisis.*" The structure of the judicial system presupposes that all judgments form droplets in a stream of thought that reflect gradual changes in societal values. Precedent is set by each and every judgment, so the conservative approach is always favored. The smallest change is considered the best. One could characterize the judicial system as risk adverse and the judiciary as the quintessential safe-keepers of the past. Judges are concerned that they not be reversed on appeal and that they not set unnecessary precedents. Their reach should not be beyond their grasp because laws that are unenforceable weaken the prestige and power of the judiciary.

How does all this apply to a litigant in a divorce action? Rulings tend to be very conservative and not creative. Persuading a judge to enter an order separating children is highly unlikely. Persuading a judge to enter an unusual parenting schedule is also unlikely. Monetary orders of support will be conservative if there is any question of ability to pay because nonpayment is a very serious matter. The judge must be convinced that the payor can meet his obligation and that he can do so without incurring further debt. Vin may have been willing to pay Mary Ann a higher amount of support than his income would have clearly justified, but the court would not require Vin to pay a support amount that might cause him to be unrealistically overextended. A father and mother may be willing to borrow money against the equity in their home in order to finance college educational costs for a child, but a court would never order a parent to do so. Yet parents may settle on such an arrangement in an agreement, and the court will approve and enter it as an uncontested judgment.

The Judicial System

The judicial system is not in the business of delivering "justice" if by that one means "an eye for an eye" or satisfactory retribution of a spouse's betrayal. The Family Courts are a place where the parties will be treated fairly in light of their current needs and circumstances and nothing more. No court can give back to the beleaguered spouse his or her earlier years or fix the personality of the "taker," to make him or her "the giver." It is astounding how often and how many clients would like the court to be the place where the just are rewarded, almost as if the court was a substitute for religious rites to "afterlife," or heaven.

Courts are first and foremost a place of business. Their job is to resolve disputes between or among people who are unable to do it themselves. It must be a safe forum; to ensure its safety many courthouses now have metal detectors and guards at the entranceway to search one's possessions, like an airport security system. Courts are like airports in another way: They are in the business of getting people where they want to go, pushing people through the system to resolution, and in the case of a failed marriage, to the land of aftermarriage. And like airports, courts have schedules to meet and spots to fill. The court docket is usually overbooked to ensure that no judicial time is wasted. The niceties of comfort, privacy, and dignity give way to the efficiency of processing cases.

Judges are held to a high degree of accountability. They must report to their chief judge the numbers of cases they have heard, decided, or that await a written decision. Statistics are kept regarding each judge's list of cases and the rapidity of disposition. The clients and the judges are cogs in the wheel of the greater system.

Judges are under a great deal of pressure to process cases. The lists of cases are long and the days grueling. The court officers want to end their days at 4:00 or 4:30 P.M. The judge wants to clear his docket. Any excuse not to hear a case today, or not at all, will be attended to closely. Lateness is not well tolerated nor is the request for special consideration based on a personal conflict. The machinery is ready to operate and tax payers' money is wasted if the courts are empty or a party is not ready to proceed.

However, unlike a business for profit, courts are run at the mercy of legislative funding. They are often woefully under-staffed and have old or malfunctioning equipment. Many judges in the Family Courts lack up-to-date computers or their own secretaries. They may be judging in temporary space without an excellent law library at their disposal. Court files are not com-puterized but are all paper, often stored in inadequate or makeshift filing systems. Most attorneys have learned to bring an extra set of papers to court in the likely event that the court's copies of the papers are missing. I have also learned to bring other reading, as it is likely that my client and I will have to wait a long time to be heard. A firm court date is never a guarantee of an actual hearing, and certainly not for the entire day as sched-uled or at the hour scheduled.

Frustration is the main feeling that permeates the court-house, frustration shared by the clients, the attorneys, and the judges. It is a vast business, poorly managed, and inevitably under-funded. Its product is something intangible but deeply important to people who almost always leave the courtroom dis-appointed with the system.

Sometimes as I stand at the bar before the presiding judge with my "brother" or "sister" attorney, I feel like we are squab-bling children currying favor from "Big Daddy." "Big Daddy" should give my side the extra slice of cake, the increased level of alimony and child support, and counsel fees as my client and I deserve this special treatment. Perhaps this is so vivid for me because it resonates with my growing up; my father was indeed a judge, and my brother and I sought his approval. Not unpre-dictably, we are both practicing lawyers, although with different areas of interest.

My attitude toward how judges reach their decisions may well have been influenced by my brilliant, thoughtful father. My brother and I watched our father write difficult opinions by first finding for one side and justifying that position, then writing a second opinion in favor of the other side. He would then sometimes try out his thoughts on the family. I doubt if the opinions of the family audience made much of an impact; however, the disciplined exercise of choosing one or another version was illuminating for my father. After rendering an opinion in a close case, my father sometimes would still wonder if he had made the wiser, fairer choice.

Close questions in the law can, by definition, go either way. A judge's personal experiences, background, character, and simple preferences play a major part in the ultimate choice. I am not proposing that judicial decisions are capricious and arbitrary, rather that they are deeply cultural, human, and personal.

Best Interests of the Child

In family law, the concept of best interests of the child is the prevailing standard for determining a child's fate in divorce. With the diversity of cultural traditions and increased sensitivity to the differences among people, the Common Law practice of applying uniform, one-size-fits-all legal constructs to the workings and unworkings of the family has come under increasing criticism.

How our cultural assumptions influence such standards as the best interests of the child can be illustrated by an analogous legal fiction in the world of tort law. In tort law, behavior is measured against the "reasonable man" standard. The concept of the reasonable man historically presumed that the person was a male of Anglo-Saxon descent, of reasonable intelligence, schooled by the community in which he was raised. Feminist thinking has focused on this prejudicial, narrow view of what is supposed to be an objective standard. Sensitivity to cultural diversity, likewise, requires us to reexamine just how useful such outdated concepts are in this complex society. Are there really commonly held beliefs about what is reasonable or in the child's best interests?

The Common Law presumed that all children could be classified in one of two ways: legitimate or illegitimate. Neither type of child had standing to speak for himself as a separate legal entity. Children required a mouthpiece. In most cases, other than family disputes, that person was usually the custodial parent. In the context of divorce, no parent could be considered suitable to serve as a mouthpiece for the child because self-interest would prevent a rational assessment of the child's needs. Only a court would have the necessary perspective to be concerned only with the child's welfare. This presumes that the court can ascertain what is best for the child. While the court may not be swayed by emotional entanglements and self-interest in the way divorcing parents might be, it is certainly swayed by the assumptions, biases, and beliefs of the particular judge.

The judge who is supposed to determine what is in a particular child's best interests is given a lengthy list of factors to consider, such as preference of the child, continuity of care, home, school, community, and access to each parent and to other family members. A judge applies his or her personally determined answer to each one. A judge does not apply a *substituted judgment standard* for finding the child's best interests, which would require the judge to consider what the child would want given the child's preference, values, and priorities. A judge will do this, for example, in cases involving termination of life, to shape a response that conforms to what the incompetent dying person might have wanted.

Children are not accorded this same deference because they are deemed incompetent by reason of age. A mature teen or a precocious younger child may have a preference that will be taken into account as one of many factors that a court must weigh. Yet the ultimate formulation remains discretionary and personal. The judge is specifically not applying the cultural norms of the family of the child but the amorphous best interests of the child. In truth, the best interests may be simply an expression of the presiding judge's own cultural preferences and values.

In cases involving Jehovah's Witnesses or Christian Scientists, the gap between a judge's cultural preference and the family's is enormously apparent. The medical care given to a child by parents who are Jehovah's Witnesses is questionable from the perspective of the greater society. The wishes of the family are intentionally disregarded in favor of some cultural norm that is held to be better for the child.

In the context of unraveling marriages and petitions to remove children from their home state, there is enormous room for discretion, and unless the judge has abused his or her discretion, the appeals court will not overturn the lower court's determination. The outcome rests on the judge's personal preferences, not those of anyone intimately connected with the family. As the variations in the cultural norms among families widen, the results have been increasingly strange as measured by the distance from marital constructs and family constructs of the family being judged.

Any Trial Is a Trial

Every trial is licensed warfare. After every trial, two terrible things have happened. The first is that the parties have said things about each other that are never forgotten nor forgiven. Worse yet, they have been said in public for the purpose of winning some advantage. The grievances held by each of the parties are now memorialized in the transcripts of the trial and emblazoned in the memory of the parties. The negative perceptions and recollections of past events have been presented as "facts" upon which the judge should rely. Few parties, when testifying in court, dwell on the positive times of the marriage or the admirable, charming traits of the former beloved. The transcript reflects a skewed recollection of the parties' past because the tale was crafted with a purpose: persuasion.

Mary Ann hardly slept or ate for days before her trial. She felt exhausted and looked haggard on the day the trial began. She looked and felt even worse when it was over. Preparation for trial is not a pleasurable experience from any perspective. I experience the same kind of anxiety one feels before an exam, conscious of everything I do not know and should have done to prepare. The similarity ends there; a trial has enormous consequences for another human being, immediately and over a lifetime.

Do trials help a divorcing couple? In the short term, they often fail to lend clarity, and in the longer term, they contaminate communication between spouses. The extra money won (or lost) comes at an enormous cost; the margin of difference between the best result and the worst result seldom justifies the emotional and litigation costs. A great "win" is usually rewarded by an appeal sought by the other side. A great loss will create the impetus for the filing of a new action.

On the whole, divorce cases do not lend themselves to the trial process. The parties are not really "plaintiffs" and "defendants" in the usual sense; they are "petitioners" seeking assistance in dividing the marital pot and setting a reasonable level of support. Unlike an ordinary civil suit, where one truly wins the whole ball of wax or walks out empty-handed, litigants in a divorce trial argue about how to allocate or assign assets and whether or not the distribution should be equal. Most importantly, former spouses must continue to deal with each other for many years following their day in court.

The present system of a full, conventional trial is not only divisive, it also is extremely cumbersome and slow. Delays to the final resolution are endless. In most jurisdictions, parties must wait a considerable period of time for the pretrial conference, a prerequisite to the trial. Only after the case has been pretried can it go on the trial list. After the trial, each side must prepare findings of fact and a proposed judgment. The court has no deadline by which it must render a decision. The gap between the hearing and receipt of the court's judgment is usually at least one to three months. However, a case may languish without decision for far longer. After the court's judgment has been entered on the docket, both sides have the right to file postjudgment motions, which can cause still more delays in the finality of the award. After postjudgment motions, either side may file a notice of appeal. It is very difficult to bring closure to the case if one side wants to protract the process. Meanwhile, the children are growing up, and time, the most precious resource, is lost.

Damage control is the name of the game in divorce. With less time expended, there will be less damage to contain and lower attorney's fees to pay. Any trial violates this cardinal principle. Protracted litigation is the single greatest contributor to the deterioration of the couple's relationship. There is always better feeling between the parties at the outset of the case. Months, even years, in the morass of the court system makes everyone cynical and increasingly mean. The best advice any divorce attorney can give is to settle quickly. If one represents the party with money, swift resolution makes sense. Time is money, and the sooner the high earner can get back to the business of producing money, the sooner he or she can be back to his prior comfort zone. The injured party will also be well served by a rapid settlement which can result in maximum guilt money.

As a result of a trial, the parties have created a distance between them that in their aftermarriage will cement the anger and lack of trust as one of the cornerstones of the new relationship. The spirit of co-operation and joint efforts for the betterment of the postmarriage may never emerge as a force or have a recognized place in the continuing relationship of the parties.

Henry and Eleanor may not have been so very much happier than Vin and Mary Ann in their good times, but they have not contaminated their past or poisoned their future, as Vin and Mary Ann did with the charges levied against each other in their respective testimony. Mary Ann charged Vin with an inability to deal honestly with their boys around money issues and personal ones. She reiterated episodes of abandonment of the children and herself during their marriage. She accused him of dishonesty and hiding money. Ginny might have had a field day with Zack's secrecy concerning business deals had they proceeded down the litigation route to trial. Moreover, had they done so, Ginny might have valued the assets properly, and Zack might have tried to use the liquidation values as he did in the mediation. The trial court would have made short shrift of Zack's ploy, and Ginny could have justified her emotional wounds from litigation on the basis of her receipt of a richer judgment than the mediated settlement rendered her. Mary Ann and Vin had less economic rationale for proceeding with a trial as the two valuations of Vin's business interest were merely thirty thousand dollars apart, an amount insufficient to justify the expense of a two-day trial.

The second unavoidable consequence of the entry of a divorce judgment is that there will now be a perceived winner and a perceived loser. This "wrong" may not only be felt poignantly by one of the parties because of the economic ramifications but more saliently because of the emotional branding of the pale of victory or loss. Perhaps the outcome will invite, as night follows day, a second war, or a revisiting of the issues in the form of postjudgment motions or an appeal. Few cases end with the entry of a divorce judgment. Nearly all that go to trial have a very active afterlife in which the parties once again try to rewrite their history. Often it is for the very same reasons that the parties were brought to the trial process that they are again trapped in the postjudgment battles. The judicial process feeds on hostility, conflict, and discord. Parties can continue fighting just about as long as one of the two decides it is in his or her interest.

Are there any circumstances where proceeding to trial makes enormous sense and is the appropriate way to resolve conflict in divorce cases? When there is an issue of removal of children from the state in which the parties resided when married and one party remains in the state, there may well be such a conflict. The impact of removing children a great distance from a parent is enormous and cannot easily be compromised. Had Natalie sought to remove the children to another state, she would have had a battle to wage with Martin. Martin might protest, and very effectively, even though as a consultant he is truly mobile. Different states treat the issue of removal of children somewhat differently. There are easier and more difficult states in which to bring a successful removal petition.

Where the valuations of a business interest, such as a closely held stock brokerage house, an oil business, or a real estate empire, are widely disparate, there is reason to go to trial, especially if the parties are unwilling to use the mean figure and the "spread" is substantial. Utilizing the same appraiser is a method of obviating this problem, but not all clients, nor their attorneys, are inclined to rely on a joint appraiser.

A trial may be the only way to resolve a case where a client refuses to accept a reasonable offer of settlement. Mary Ann could be viewed as such a client. In effect, she insisted on litigation without any rational reason for this choice other than she was not prepared to end the marriage without an opportunity to speak her pain, distress, and heartbreak. The facts of her case did not justify a trial when measured by the legal expense, the result obtained (less favorable than the settlement offer), and the cost of the court's time. Mary Ann felt compelled to fight even if in so doing she only gained the right to live on a lesser amount of alimony and confirm by action her painful experience of losing Vin.

In terms of the quality of aftermarriage following a trial, there can be nothing but grief and recrimination. Each litigant has wounds to nurse, aggravated by the memory of injustices uttered and arguments not made. The relationship of the once loving couple has inevitably deteriorated past all levels that either party had anticipated at the commencement of the divorce action. A trial cements for the parties the fact that they are enemies. They have fought on different sides in a public forum. The carnage of the event is palpable and distressing even for a casual observer. One cannot imagine that the warring couple will ever be able to discuss, without heat, sharing children, arranging and attending together graduations and weddings, or sitting in a hospital room, tensely awaiting the outcome of their child's operation.

CHAPTER 14

Realignment in Aftermarriage

The need to learn how to realign within a relationship survives the formal end of marriage. In fact, it is a skill that may be even more important in the transition from marriage to aftermarriage and during aftermarriage than in an intact marriage. Now the couple must analyze and come to grips with their different definitions of divorce and divorce behavior after having failed to align their marital constructs.

Many divorced couples face the task of realignment in aftermarriage without adequate preparation or guidance. They are the same couples who were unable to realign satisfactorily their expectations during an ongoing marriage. Realignment in aftermarriage is a far more complex undertaking than in an intact marriage. Shared history, children, and obligations define the bonds. Separate residences define the distance. There is no established roadmap or universally adopted conventions for this phase of aftermarriage. Each unhappy aftermarriage is unhappy in its own way.

Legal rules and religious traditions are ominously silent. The legal system has no postdivorce laws that address the expected conduct of ex-spouses other than sanctions for noncompliance with financial obligations and a prohibition against removal of a child from the home state without court permission. There is no religious code that instructs ex-spouses to honor and cherish each other or offers a set of customs to follow. Where can people learn realistic expectations of aftermarriage behavior?

Everybody contemplating divorce has some idea of how they expect to relate to their former spouse. Even those who do accept that divorce will not sever all ties would admit that they expect the post-divorce relationship to be substantially different from the marital relationship.

The ideas which divorcing people start with might be labeled their *aftermarriage construct,* paralleling the marital construct. The aftermarriage construct, like the marital construct, is a set of ideas culled from religious beliefs, legal traditions, culture, popular literature and film, personal experience, and conscious and unconscious notions. I do not think that most people going through a divorce have ever articulated for themselves, much less for their spouse, their ideas, hopes, and emotional and practical expectations of how aftermarriage will be managed by the newly configured family. Nor have they thought sufficiently about the rearranged family's necessary evolution and likely expansion. Most people stop in their analysis of expectations with the event of divorce. They do not anticipate the necessity of multiple realignments of the spousal relationship, of the rearranged family to the extended families, and of the divorced spouses with friends and professionals (teachers and doctors, for example).

As a family lawyer, I do not necessarily hear from my clients after the divorce is final and the paperwork that follows the final decree has been completed. However, in many cases, our contact continues over many years, even decades. The clients that return do so because of a variety of reasons, each illustrating the continuing, endless connection of former spouses. Former spouses return because of one or more of the following: substantial change of circumstances necessitating a modification (loss of employment, increase in income, remarriage and request for modification of alimony and/or child support); petition for removal of children to another state; failure to pay support; request for review of support in light of retirement; request for review of college obligation in light of parties' current circumstances; purchase or sale of the marital home or another home; a will, necessitated by divorce or remarriage; a prenuptial agreement; and other anticipated or unanticipated events in the lives of the rearranged family.

The experiences of the central five couples (Vin and Mary Ann, Henry and Eleanor, Martin and Natalie, Mark and Bettina, and Zack and Ginny) illustrate some of the problems of aftermarriage and situations that require realignment.

Mary Ann and Vin's Aftermarriage

Unfortunately, Mary Ann and Vin were in the 5 percent who litigated their divorce, and their aftermarriage was forever colored by that experience. Whenever Vin is a day late in his support payment, Mary Ann calls me, after having left threatening messages of further court action on Vin's answering machine. I know that Mary Ann struggles with her impulse for revenge and sees further court action as a way of reminding Vin of the pain he caused her and the boys.

Vin feels cornered by circumstances, financial and emotional. He is surprised and disappointed that he feels some of the same confining ties to Mary Ann as he felt before the divorce. Only now those ties are court ordered obligations which he may not flout without facing contempt. He is even more resentful of the ways in which his earlier decision to marry and have children with Mary Ann has ensnared him for life. He had wanted to divorce in order to walk away from his past, but the marital bonds maintain remarkable vitality in aftermarriage. He owes half his paycheck to his ex-wife and feels that his net financial worth is a pittance, especially compared to what he had owned before it all began. The condo mortgage remains his liability as do the escalating bills from his sons' Ivy League colleges.

What has changed for Vin or Mary Ann? They are even more deeply mired in their financial woes and now distrust each other. Mary Ann lives alone in the large condo, only intermittently shared with one, or both, boys. It is on the market but has not sold (the price may need to be dropped far below the mortgage they still owe). Mary Ann feels rejected, disposable, and replaced. Vin can spend day and night with his office manager, Jill. But they live on a tight budget with little money for amusements. Many evenings are spent fending off Mary Ann's phone calls or worrying about the numerous expenses of the boys.

Vin does not miss going home to Mary Ann. Every day he is grateful for his energetic relationship with his younger companion. But he has less than a new life, if new is defined as a fresh start. Unlike a bankruptcy, a divorce can seldom confer a fresh start. Mary Ann's life is far worse than it had been, and she is powerless to alter that fact. With time, she has adopted a less desperate attitude. There are days that she is grateful to have excellent health, kind and caring children, and a job she still enjoys. Like a widow, she has coped with the loss and found new strengths within herself. She feels much more her own person, albeit sadder and more lonely than when she had the assumed security of an intact marriage.

A year after the final divorce judgment was rendered, I received a disturbing call from Mary Ann. Unlike earlier calls, her voice was not strident, but somber and quiet. She reported that their younger boy had dropped out of college and was clinically depressed. What could she do to help her son? How would his leaving college affect her situation? What steps could she take to make Vin deal with this? He never took her calls, at home or work. He never wanted to hear from her. Mary Ann had left numerous messages on his various machines; she had written to him, but Vin did not reply. Was there anything that I could do to reach Vin so that they could work as a team to deal with this? Their younger son had moved back to the condo. He hardly talked and lay idly about in his darkened bedroom. Mary Ann was beside herself with worry and fear for his welfare.

Since the divorce, Vin has had great difficulty maintaining any meaningful relationship with the boys. The boys felt loyal and protective of their frail mother. Mary Ann, in her uncontrollable disappointment, had unwittingly alienated the boys from their father. Although she believed that she had encouraged them to see their father, she also raised the boys' anxiety by peppering them with questions, "Has Dad been to see you at college or is he too busy with his new life? Did Dad finally pay the overdue college tuition bill so that you could re-enroll this spring, or did he just say that he would get to it when he had time and money?"

Vin believed he had reached out often to the boys but got only monosyllabic responses, especially when they were staying at the condo. The boys shied away from him, particularly around tuition times because they did not want to get caught in the middle, nor did they want to discuss their own concerns about Vin's ability to pay. Neither son knew how to talk to his father about the rearranged family, its distressing dynamics, or his personal pain. Vin did not know how to address his altered relationship with his sons, either.

The stress of Vin and Mary Ann's aftermarriage relationship, combined with the financial stresses, has contaminated all the family dynamics. Even children of college age need the security of knowing that their parents can communicate effectively with each other about their needs, their education, and their future.

I called Vin's attorney to speak about the younger son's situation. While Vin's attorney was sympathetic, neither he nor I could alleviate the pain of the situation in any meaningful way. We agreed to suggest to our respective clients that they work together to get their son medical treatment as soon as possible. The judgment of divorce obligated Vin to maintain medical insurance for the family, so a few therapy sessions would be covered. No one believed that a few sessions would suffice; but without parental cooperation, it might be difficult to arrange more.

Mary Ann and Vin knew that they needed to work together to face this turn of events. However, each parent secretly blamed the other for the present calamity. If only the parents could put aside their recent ugly past and fully cooperate, then their son would have his best chance to regain emotional stability and rekindle his desire to succeed.

No court process can mandate this outcome. No mediator or attorney can manufacture a viable aftermarriage relationship. The only people who have that power are the divorcing couple. They must get past their disappointment, pain, hurt, and anger in order to parent effectively. Effective parenting requires facing the daunting task of realignment of personal aftermarriage constructs and finding ways of accommodating differences. Failure to do so invites disaster.

Mary Ann and Vin might have constructively realigned their relationship in aftermarriage if they could have compartmentalized their relationship, separating finances and blame from legitimate parental concerns. They needed to resolve to never speak about their past, their trial, or their failings. Oral communication should have been limited to one topic only: the present and future best interests, welfare, and emotional needs of their children. All other concerns, such as financial issues, should have been reduced to writing and mailed to the other parent (and certainly not given to a son to deliver).

Restricting oral communication to narrowly and carefully defined parameters of appropriate discourse would have reopened some channel of communication after litigation. Issues of support and educational expenses could have been addressed, without prejudice, in writing. Had these simple rules of behavior been adopted by Vin and Mary Ann as essential ingredients of their aftermarriage conduct, they might have been able to unite in their shared desire for their son's speedy recovery.

Henry and Eleanor's Aftermarriage

The other classic couple, Henry and Eleanor, who arrived at a negotiated settlement, met with far fewer aftermarriage problems. Nevertheless, they, as all divorced couples, did not escape the need for significant realignment of family arrangements.

In the short term, very little really changed after the divorce for Henry and Eleanor, other than that they had separate primary residences. They had the financial resources to maintain their individual lifestyles, even with the extra expense of an apartment for Henry closer to the college. Henry continued to do the work he always did and just as avidly. Eleanor was free to explore the singles scene as was Henry, assuming he had an urge to do so. Maybe with time, one of them would find another person with whom to share love and life. Statistically, Henry's chances of meeting a companion were far better than Eleanor's, and his opportunities were greater than hers in his present lifestyle. Eleanor was isolated in the suburban house and did not have many contacts likely to introduce her to available men. Unless a middle-aged, divorced person reconnects with a friend from the past, any new acquaintance will lack an historical connection.

Shared children are unlikely, just as is shared knowledge of each other's family of origin. The force and the length of the couples' "history" together can hardly ever be replicated.

Eleanor and Henry celebrated the holidays together with their children for several years after the day of divorce. The after-marriage family was united on many of their children's events: birthdays, college graduations, marriages, and the births of their grandchildren. They were no longer "married" in the legal meaning nor did they dwell under the same roof, as most married people do, but in critical ways remained closely connected. Almost without fail and instinctively, they shared with each other their good and bad news. They continued to treat each other with respect and a spirit of cooperation, the hallmark of their earlier relationship.

They proceeded this way for four years. And then Henry was offered a more prestigious appointment at higher compensation from a university located in another state. Henry's relocation triggered the need for a more substantial realignment than the divorce had caused. Strangely, or perhaps not so strangely, Henry's move brought Eleanor unexpected pain and belated grieving. Now she had really lost an important piece of her marriage—physical proximity to Henry. They could no longer pretend to themselves or with their children that nothing had changed. The increased physical distance did not cause either Henry or Eleanor to express any more or less emotion directly to each other. However, the reality was that they saw far less of each other and no longer knew as much about each other's lives. Telephone calls dwindled in length, frequency, and, more importantly, in meaningful content. Their connection grew attenuated and not as relevant to daily life as it had been. The children and grandchildren now visited with them separately, and major holidays had to be allocated, rather than shared, in aftermarriage.

Experiencing the impact of aftermarriage at some time after the divorce, even a long time after, is not uncommon. Often the homework necessary for successful realignment only happens because of relocation or the introduction of a new person into the rearranged family. Sometimes it even awaits the death of a family member. The genuine watershed event for many couples may follow long after the initial steps of unraveling an intact marriage have been taken, particularly for those couples who participated in a successful mediation. A tranquil ending of an intact marriage often postpones the task of realignment and masks the scope of the undertaking. There are some couples who avoid the work of realignment by behaving as if they were still married but have chosen to live separately. On the other end of the spectrum, are the couples who elect litigation, thereby irreversibly altering their aftermarriage relationship.

Martin and Natalie's Aftermarriage

The companion couple, Martin and Natalie, illustrates other complexities of realignment, which emerged soon after the day of divorce, despite their having reached a negotiated settlement agreement.

Natalie experienced aftermarriage as anything but the fresh start she had anticipated. She and Martin ultimately avoided litigation with the help of a parent-coordinator (a therapist, specializing in children of divorce), who was also named in the parties' settlement agreement. The initial accord was reached only after Martin stopped insisting on staying in the house and Natalie recognized that the children enjoyed extended time with their father.

After the judge allowed their agreement, Natalie and Martin spoke on the phone or emailed one another, nearly daily—or so it seemed to Natalie. With the passage of several years, the frequency has been reduced because the children do more of their own negotiating with each parent. But hardly a day went by that the parents did not have to consider each other, even if only in the context of their child-rearing partnership. Natalie redecorated the house after Martin departed. She made many new friends and vacationed with, and without, the children in new settings. But it was amazing to her how often she had to contact Martin about some issue or other.

Natalie began dating a wonderful man, whom her family really liked and considered much more her "equal" in brainpower, ambition, and life goals. Yet Natalie still felt altogether too involved with Martin to be ready to truly partner again. There just was not enough time, energy, and space in her life to accommodate a full-time male partner. Natalie and her "significant other" saw a lot of each other but maintained separate residences. Martin became involved with a lovely single woman who moved in with him. When the children were with Martin, the four of them spent family time together. The children liked Martin's girlfriend but regretted that Natalie did not also live there. Martin, his girlfriend, and Natalie had a strange, rearranged, marriage-like relationship that now resembled the three-legged marriage or complex marriage. Natalie felt she had a remote husband/involved father in Martin and a lover in her "significant other." Martin felt that he had two wives and two children. And the children felt that they had three adults to whom they could turn. Life for all of them was simpler before. Was simpler better? On quiet winter nights, Natalie and Martin, from time to time, thought that way, but the die had been cast and the land of aftermarriage is where they now resided. The only question was whether either would have the interest, desire, and energy to commit to someone new and reenact the dance of legally sanctioned coupling.

Natalie and Martin found themselves perpetually involved in realigning their former relationship in light of the ever-changing needs of their own lives and their children's lives. At the outset, Natalie tried to control how Martin parented the children during his time with them. She wanted the children properly fed, as defined by her nutritional standards. She wanted homework time and bedtime to be at the same hour as in her home. After many months and with the guidance of the parent coordinator, Natalie learned to back off from these demands.

As their daughter, Nicole, moved into her teens, the mother/daughter relationship became increasingly strained. Nicole wanted to spend more time at her father's home, and Natalie hated having to accept this not unforeseeable, adolescent developmental change. Natalie did not want to realign the parent/child relationship; she wanted Martin's help in muzzling their daughter's expression of any such preference. He was less than accommodating, especially because the children had become even more important to him and to his self-definition since the divorce, a commonly experienced shift in priorities. Fortunately for both Natalie and the children, Martin did not go to court to seek a child support order from Natalie, even though he now hosted the children at his home 56 percent of the time. Martin may have kept track, but he was wise enough not to translate his mathematical calculations into action that would have caused the children distress for very short financial gain.

Other differences in child rearing philosophies flowered as the children aged. Life experiences and new friends influenced both Martin and Natalie; their memories of how they had parented together waned. Martin and his girlfriend marched to a different drummer than Natalie and her boyfriend. The idea of a fixed schedule and discipline were anathema in Martin's home, whereas they were central themes in Natalie's. The place and importance of money saved, or spent, were different in the two homes.

This last distinction became a critical one as their elder child, Michael, reached his senior year of high school. The negotiated settlement agreement, signed by Martin and Natalie, provided that, "the parties would negotiate in good faith their respective college obligations in light of their then current financial circumstances, including all assets, debts, and income." Martin had not saved any money since the parties' divorce, nor had he set aside any college funds for Michael's education. Martin thought a state college would be fine for Michael, just as it had been fine for him. His parents had not paid for his education; he thought that the costs of private college education were exorbitant in light of its benefits. Natalie did not share his perspective on the relative benefits of private college versus state college. She wanted Michael to go to "the best" college, and she believed that they should contribute equally to their son's education. Disagreements regarding the cost/benefit analysis of public versus private education are typical of many couples, be they married or formerly married. Individual priorities do not disappear or realign perfectly because of a piece of paper.

Natalie and Martin learned that realignment in aftermarriage required enormous flexibility, accommodation, compromise, and a forgiving attitude toward irreconcilable differences. Regardless of where their son attended college, the parenting coordinator counseled each parent to respect the other's philosophy. When Natalie sought a consultation with me on "the college issue," I reminded her of the grave potential harm to Michael, were she and Martin to litigate the allocation of his college costs. Parents who cannot adjust to their inevitable and irreconcilable differences sow destructive seeds for themselves and their children in aftermarriage.

Mark and Bettina's Aftermarriage

Mark and Bettina, the protectorate couple, did not discuss in advance how they wanted their aftermarriage to be. Mark knew that he wanted his relationship with Bettina to end. He did not want her to think of him as a friend she could call upon whenever a need arose. He would do all that he was supposed to do and do it in a very civilized manner, but that was all. Bettina hated to lose contact with anyone, and that included any friend and most acquaintances. Their aftermarriage realignment followed Mark's wishes. In aftermarriage, as in any relationship, no one can insist on another's love or a genuinely caring relationship.

Mark did not wait long to take the plunge after his divorce; he consciously chose not to replicate a protectorate marriage bargain. He remarried within 18 months of the uncontested divorce hearing. His second wife became pregnant within the first year of marriage, and Mark had the family he had always wanted. He and Bettina never spoke; he did not think about her daily or even monthly. He did notice in the local paper that Bettina's mother had died and, only on this one occasion, wrote her a note. For Mark, the land of aftermarriage was free of all marital bonds except the monthly alimony check to Bettina, which was direct-deposited to Bettina's account, so there was never a problem with lateness or missed payments. He did not feel the squeeze too terribly since the HMO had increased his salary substantially in the last two years.

Bettina's standard of living after divorce was different, but she was painting every day and had a man in her life, who adored her. He was much older than Bettina, and 20 years Mark's senior. He had his family and was most appreciative of Bettina's sweet personality and presence in his life.

For this couple, realignment meant a complete severance of their relationship, except for automatic monthly checks. Bettina and Mark have moved away from each other and toward new and intimate relationships. They were not unaffected by their failed marriage, but each was relatively young (early 40s), resilient, and unencumbered. They were able to redesign another marriage, or marriage-like, relationship. Bettina's relationship was again a protectorate one; she was the grateful receiver and adorer. Mark chose a classic marriage model.

The lack of enduring connections between Mark and Bettina, such as children or a very long-term marriage, meant that Mark could proceed with his new classic marriage bargain without having Bettina as a palpable, omnipresent silent partner. Similarly, Bettina was free to move fully into the new relationship with her older protector, undisturbed by interactions with Mark. Mark was grateful for the joy of a full family, and Bettina felt well loved by her older protector, who truly welcomed hearing her opinions and innermost thoughts.

Zack and Ginny's Aftermarriage

The complex marital bargain couple, Zack and Ginny, present yet another twist to realignment opportunities and possible resolutions. Ginny contacted me only once, and very briefly, after we parted ways. She said that she understood better why I had advised her to be more assertive about her interest in the marital property. Yet she had no regrets about the financial outcome. What had really mattered to her was that she and Zack remained on good terms in aftermarriage, and they were. I learned some of the following directly from Ginny, but the rest is simply my own intuition.

Zack and Ginny had a three-legged marriage. They found ways of reforming "complex" three-legged marriage-like relationships with new people, but as was characteristic of their marriage, each remained a significant player in the other's newly formed triangle. Even though Zack and Ginny had formally divorced, they continued their individual patterns in an unchanged manner; this time the third leg of the stool was the former spouse and not a stranger. True intimacy could never really happen for them until they engaged in self-examination aimed at breaking their personal patterns. Zack and Ginny were now each other's unacknowledged partners—a new role for each of them in their respective lives. Zack used Ginny for solace when his girlfriend treated him harshly, regularly escaping to Ginny's city apartment to get some space from the intensity of that relationship. Ginny spent time with several men and thought of Zack as "her family," someone she could really count on and with whom she could really connect. The dances of the earlier marriage were replicated with a partially new cast, different roles, but the same tunes played.

Ginny and Zack illustrate how difficult a profound change in habits and patterns may be without some kind of intervention other than legal. The vast majority of people who have changed profoundly, deeply, and meaningfully are only those who did the necessary internal examination, and that may not occur just by moving from marriage to aftermarriage. It involves taking the time, energy, and space to understand oneself, one's origins, and assumptions about love, intimacy, marriage, self-esteem, and boundaries of self. It also involves learning, or relearning, the significance of one's own marital construct and the concept of alignment and/or realignment.

Expectations Revisited

As I write these aftermarriage scenarios, I hope that I am writing an accurate distillation of what I have observed from my vantage point, rather than a caricature of the cycles. The divorced people who have constructively moved forward with their lives in an insightful and free way are circumscribed; they are the people who, in aftermarriage, have done the arduous and painful homework of self-examination or have emerged from a childless marriage or a marriage where successful realignment in aftermarriage has been brokered. They are also the people who know how to welcome, even embrace, change and attract good luck.

The young and childless couples are the most objectively free to move forward. Couples with grown children are also less saddled by marital baggage, although they still carry a history. They can, in theory, change more than their living arrangements but are trapped by reduced flexibility. Some older divorced people redesign their lives in remarkable ways: They change location or jobs or explore a new or forgotten interest or former friend.

Couples with young children, sapped by work and parental responsibilities, have the least capacity and energy to remake their lives from the inside out. Just as when immersed in the intact marriage, the land of aftermarriage offers no relief from the stress of this stage of life. In fact, aftermarriage only magnifies the financial woes and emotional scars. Additionally, the divorce process has created more baggage to transport to the next relationship. Despite this unnerving truth, I have seen many people find great happiness in aftermarriage, with or without remarriage. Flexibility and understanding of one's own and one's partner's marital and aftermarriage constructs have been key concepts in unlocking the passageway to greater serenity.

Planning for Aftermarriage

I try to educate my clients about the potential problem areas and realignment issues in aftermarriage. As I explain what divorced people usually do about attending school conference functions, doctor's appointments, graduations, and so on, I sense that many have their own ideas of what is "normal" and that I, myself, am making a subjective judgment of the norm.

While some divorced parents can easily manage a joint school conference, I do not assume that to be true, especially if the scheduled conference follows a trial or court appearance. Meeting together with a child's teacher is desirable from everyone's perspective, but it could be too uncomfortable or painful for one, or both, parents. Nevertheless, a custodial parent must tell the other parent about such a meeting and let them make up their own mind about attending. A custodial parent's comfort level is always of tertiary importance when compared to the need of the other parent to be invited to attend and the best interest of the child, which is met when there are two involved parents. This example may seem trivial, but it illustrates that right and wrong in aftermarriage are not totally unchartered waters or just a matter of personal preference. The comfort and/or preference of a custodial parent is not the primary consideration; the best interest of the child is paramount.

To the extent possible, I urge couples to talk with each other not just about getting a divorce but also about how they want aftermarriage to be, as early in the process as possible. Couples should discuss a wide range of topics. Child sharing and its practical details are the most significant and may well be the hardest. One might begin with easier topics like future family events, such as graduations, weddings, and deaths, then move on to aspirations about the future emotional connections that they hope to maintain with the other.

Divorcing couples should imagine themselves 1, 5, and 10 years in the future. How would they like to behave toward each other? What rules of conduct in aftermarriage would they like to propose? How do they want to communicate? If these questions can be anticipated and addressed, then the divorcing couple's expectations of their aftermarriage relationship might be realistic and constructive, based upon understanding each other's preferences (even if not based on experience). Such an aftermarriage agreement would not contain any legal jargon or reference to assets and support. It would focus entirely on what future events the couple will face and how they will cope with them in light of their own interests, their children's, and their family traditions.

Couples might think of such an agreement as a safety net for their children. The children's welfare will remain uppermost in both parents' minds, despite whatever conflicts exist between them or drove them apart. Their children will know that even if the marriage has terminated, both parents will honor some family traditions and be there for them at critical events. Through such an agreement, parents can anticipate and prepare for predictable and unpredictable events in their children's lives that will require a team effort. They will have had an opportunity to discuss meaningfully how to bridge future differences in child-rearing philosophies. Without any prior consideration of predictable future mine fields, their yet to be "teenagers" will have a field day manipulating each parent around such issues as curfews, dating, driving, and so on.

If possible, parents should discuss and then memorialize their educational philosophies, particularly with respect to the value of private education versus public education at the secondary and college level as well as college savings plans and financial aid opportunities for their children's future education. Couples might think ahead to the advantages and disadvantages of a child working while in college, assuming that a choice exists. They might also speak to their aspirations for education beyond the college level for their children, particularly if they have enjoyed such higher education.

An agreement that memorializes all these aspects of a couple's aftermarriage construct will be a roadmap to what they can, and cannot, expect from their former spouse. They can provide meaningful assurances of future conduct to each other, their children, family and friends, professionals, and other third parties that will be honored, regardless of their physical separation and any lingering emotional pain. They will have taken care of the most important issues and can see to their own healing in their own time.

The task of talking together about an aftermarriage agreement, much less memorializing it, may well be beyond the grasp of most divorcing couples. Yet, I would urge you to think about how you might want such an agreement to read, were it possible to discuss its terms with your spouse or ex-spouse. Engaging in this exercise will clarify your position on these common aftermarriage issues, so that you can deal with them more effectively when they arise.

The Aftermarriage Agreement: Understandings and Aspirations

Events

- ❖ All teacher conferences and doctor and dentist appointments shall be scheduled at a time known to both parents.
- ❖ Neither parent shall fail to inform the other parent in advance of any such appointment.
- ❖ Both parents may attend all appointments.
- ❖ Both parents are to be informed of all children's performances, games, or music recitals.
- ❖ Both parents will make best efforts to attend all children's performances.
- ❖ Children's birthday parties will be held at the marital residence.

❖ The following events shall be celebrated jointly:

_____

_____

_____

_____

❖ The following events shall be celebrated separately:

_____

_____

_____

_____

❖ Grandparents, aunts, uncles, cousins on both sides will be included/excluded from ...

_____

_____

_____

_____

Children's Expenses

The following children's expenses shall be incurred only after consultation:

❖ Children's allowances
❖ Automobile purchase, maintenance, and insurance
❖ Computer purchases
❖ Wedding expenses

Communication

❖ The parties commit to communicating at least once a month to discuss the children.
❖ Neither parent shall call the other at work, except in an emergency.

❖ Communication shall happen by … (Mode).

❖ Resolution of child related conflicts: [Procedure]

❖ Scheduling of vacation: [Procedure]

❖ Introduction of persons of the opposite sex in the parents lives: [Procedure; timing; overnights]

Aspirations for the Children

❖ Private college education

❖ Education beyond college

❖ Continuation of lessons in …

❖ Summer employment for children while in high school/college

❖ Part-time jobs during school year while in high school/college

Communication with Former Relatives and Joint Friends

❖ Relationship of husband and wife to each others' relatives

❖ Understandings about how to share joint friends

Aspirations for Aftermarriage Relationship

❖ Lovers but no longer married

❖ Friends but not lovers

❖ Civilized but not truly friendly

❖ Minimal communication

❖ No communication

This list represents merely a sample of the topics and concerns that might be included in an aftermarriage agreement. Preparing such a list will highlight points of accord and discord that the traditional legal process largely disregards but which are often the stuff of real conflict and/or disappointment in aftermarriage. The myth of divorce covers only a limited understanding of the experience of aftermarriage. These issues, and any others you come up with that will need hammering out, are what your divorce judgment *did not* resolve, but issues that you will need to if you want to minimize emotional tribulations for yourselves and your children in your aftermarriage.

In Closing

This book has presented the proposition that all marriages with children and all long marriages, happy or unhappy, contain the prospect of a lengthy aftermarriage. Except in short, childless marriages, marital and parental responsibilities endure. Conceiving of the relationship following divorce as aftermarriage acknowledges the reality that once-married couples will always be connected in some fashion. The myth of divorce has encouraged harmful, false expectations. The concept of aftermarriage explains and prepares spouses for the necessary realignment of their relationship.

Myths surround marriage as well as divorce. In this book, you have learned about the five types of marriage bargains that may provide handles to grasp how marriages—your marriage—might be classified and understood, particularly in the context of the divorce fiction. Becoming knowledgeable about the nature of the institution of marriage from a legal perspective, including its contractual and partnership aspects, may empower you to face the challenges of aftermarriage more successfully. I also hope you will think afresh about the sanctity of parenthood and disentangle your definitions and expectations of marriage from your parental responsibilities. The legal fiction of divorce has engendered demeaning classifications, such as primary custodial parent and visiting parent. Understanding that divorce is a part of marriage, and that which follows is aftermarriage may encourage greater wisdom and more constructive solutions.